Christoph Schwöbel is Lecturer in
Systematic Theology and Director of the
Research Institute in Systematic Theology,
King's College, University of London.

Colin E. Gunton is Professor of Christian
Doctrine at King's College, University of
London.

PERSONS, DIVINE AND HUMAN

PERSONS, DIVINE AND HUMAN

KING'S COLLEGE ESSAYS IN THEOLOGICAL ANTHROPOLOGY

Edited by
Christoph Schwöbel and Colin E. Gunton
for the
Research Institute in Systematic Theology

T&T CLARK
EDINBURGH

T&T CLARK
59 GEORGE STREET
EDINBURGH EH2 2LQ
SCOTLAND

BT
701.2
.P4250
1991

First Published 1991

ISBN 0 567 09584 3

British Library Cataloguing in Publication Data

A catalogue record for this book
is available from the British Library

Typeset by Trinity Typesetting, Edinburgh
Printed and bound in Great Britain by Billing & Sons Ltd, Worcester

Contents

Introduction

by Christoph Schwöbel

I

When R. J. Illingworth delivered his Bampton Lectures for the year 1894 under the title *Personality — Human and Divine* this choice of topic was highly indicative for the growing conviction among philosophers of religion and theologians that the concepts of person and personality provided the central focus for theological and philosophical reflection. This conviction, which was programmatically expressed in the symposium *Personal Idealism*, published in 1902, is tersely stated in Illingworth's summary of the principal thesis of his lectures:

> Their main contention is that, whereas physical science has nowise weakened, critical philosophy has distinctly strengthened the claim — the immemorial claim of human personality, to be a spiritual thing; and as such the highest category under which we can conceive of God.[1]

In Illingworth's argument this claim has many facets, some philosophical, some theological. Personality is in his personalist modification of absolute idealism 'the gateway through which all knowledge must inevitably pass'[2] in science as well as in philosophy; it is the 'inevitable and necessary starting-point of all human thought'.[3] Moreover, Illingworth argues that personality 'is also our canon of reality, the most real thing we know, and by comparison with which we estimate the amount of reality in other things'.[4]

The reality and the understanding of personality, which is described as the synthetic unity of reason, will and love, is, according to Illingworth, indissolubly bound up with Christianity; 'the advent of Christianity', he writes, 'created a new epoch both in the development and recognition of human personalty'.[5]

---

[1] R. J. Illingworth, *Personality—Human and Divine, being the Bampton Lectures for 1894* (London: Macmillan, 1894), pp. VII-VIII.

[2] *Ibid.* p. 25.

[3] *Ibid.* p. 41.

[4] *Ibid.* p. 43.

[5] *Ibid.* p. 8.

The Incarnation, for Illingworth the event in which 'human nature [had] in a unique instance been personally united to God' and in which 'the whole human race, whether male or female, barbarian or Scythian, bond or free, were declared capable of a communicated participation in that union', had secured the universality of an all-inclusive conception of personality as the essence of what it means to be human. And it had through 'the holiness which this union demanded' also set a new standard of the unity of human personhood which 'admitted of no dualism'.[6] The Incarnation provides for Illingworth the foundation for a subsequent conception of human personality and of divine personality which found its exemplary expression in the patristic theologians and, as far as human personality is concerned, its decisive exposition in the thought of Augustine, Luther and Kant.

The understanding of both human personality and of divine personhood are for Illingworth irreducibly trinitarian. Human personality is 'essentially triune, not because its chief functions are three — thought, desire and will — for they might conceivably be more, but because it consists of a subject, an object, and their relation'.[7] This idealist account of the triune conception of human self-consciousness is in Illingworth's understanding also the root of the social character of human personality which in the process of the realization of its potentiality forms personal relationships with others. The constitution of divine personhood can also only be expressed in trinitarian terms. Illingworth summarizes his analogical argument in the following form:

> Our own personality is triune; but it is a potential, unrealized triunity, which is incomplete in itself, and must go beyond itself for completion, as, for example, in the family. If, therefore, we are to think of God as personal, it must be by what is called the method of eminence (via eminentiae) — the method, that is, which considers God as possessing, in transcendent perfection, the same attributes which are imperfectly possessed by man. He must, therefore, be pictured as One whose triunity has nothing potential or unrealized about it; whose triune elements are eternally actualized, by no outward influence, but from within; a Trinity in Unity; a social God with all the conditions of personal existence internal to Himself.[8]

Building on this groundwork Illingworth presents his 'cumulative argument'[9] for the existence of a personal God, in which he

---

[6] *Ibid.* p. 12.
[7] *Ibid.* p. 69.
[8] *Ibid.* p. 71-5.
[9] Illingworth (*ibid.* p. 84) quotes John Caird's *Introduction to the Philosophy of Religion*, p. 133.

analyzes the four main traditional theistic proofs — cosmological, teleological, ontological and moral — not as demonstrations, but as 'an analysis of the unconscious or implicit logic of religion, as tracing the steps of the process by which the human spirit rises to the knowledge of God'. In addition, he considers the arguments from the investigation of religion in the 'prehistoric period' and in 'pre-Christian history', before he discusses the cumulative force of his arguments in the lecture with the title: 'Jesus Christ — the Divine and Human Person'. The Incarnation provides the cornerstone for his argument that human personality offers the decisive insight into the existence and nature of a personal God, not because the triune constitution of human personhood is the basis for the projection of the triune being of God, but because the Incarnation reveals the perfect being of God as the 'archetype'[10] of humanity's potential being: 'Thus the actual Trinity of God explains the potential trinity of man; and our anthropomorphic language follows from our theomorphic minds.'[11]

Reflection on the character of personhood has lost nothing of its relevance since Illingworth's days, although not many would be able to share his conviction that the spiritual nature of personhood has been so amply demonstrated by critical philosophy that it provided an utterly persuasive starting-point for the validation of claims about the existence of God and for the elucidation of God's personal being. While Illingworth and many of his contemporaries believed they could perceive a convergence of thinking on the nature of human personality which pointed to its inextricable link with divine personhood and its appearance in history in the Incarnation, we are today confronted with a sometimes bewildering diversity of conceptions of personhood developed from a variety of perspectives, differing not only with regard to the material understanding of what it means to be a person, but also with regard to the status of personhood in our conceptual and practical interaction with one another and with the world.

Materialism which, as Illingworth thought at the end of the 19th century to have been shown to be an untenable explanation of personality,[12] has in the 20th century experienced a significant flourishing, especially with regard to its claim to explain the phenomena of personhood — from the early programmatic statements of 'behaviourism' shortly before the First World War to the elaborate theoretical constructions of 'Sociobiology' today. Its strongest support is the all-inclusive claim made for (not always

[10] *Ibid.* p. XIII.
[11] *Ibid.* p. 214.
[12] *Cf. ibid.* p. 48-53.

by) the physical sciences that everything is ultimately subject to scientific explanation in terms of the causal interrelationships of matter. Where this claim is couched in terms of a general statement of universal application, that scientific explanation can give a complete account of everything in terms of the forms of organisation of matter, its reductionist character becomes apparent. Persons, personal identity, freedom, communion and consciousness are ultimately seen as the random products of physical processes on high levels of organization whose true character is disguised by treating persons and personal phenomena under a category *sui generis*.[13]

On the other hand, some of the most recent attempts at offering a philosophical account of the structure of personhood have revived radical forms of Cartesian dualism as, it is claimed, the most coherent conception of personal identity.[14] Here the ancient concept of the soul is reintroduced to describe human persons as constituted in a dual structure consisting of body and soul. The soul is understood as the conscious substratum of all mental acts, which can in no way be reduced to physical states and their properties, though they interact with the body in such a way that they determine the brain-states which are the correlates to the beliefs and desires which make up the structure of the soul. Furthermore, since it is logically possible that the conscious life of the mental structure which is designated by the term 'soul' continues even when its present body ceases to exist, there is — this is the 'simple argument'[15] — actually a conscious substantial entity, the soul, which provides the ultimate reference-point for personal identity.

Between these two views, which define the perimeters of the debate, there is a rich variety of views neither committed to the stark materialism of the reductionism of scientism nor the radical dualism of Neo-Cartesian views. The pluriformity of views of life in modern societies presents us not only with a variety of contemporary intellectual approaches for the understanding of

---

[13]   *Cf.* the instructive and provocative paper 'Purposeless People' by Peter Atkins, in: A. R. Peacocke, G. Gillett (eds.), *Persons and Personality: A Contemporary Enquiry* (Oxford: Basil Blackwell, 1987), pp. 12-36.

[14]   *Cf.* e.g. Richard Swinburne, *The Evolution of the Soul* (Oxford: Clarendon Press, 1986) and H. D. Lewis, *The Elusive Mind* (London: Allen & Unwin, 1969).

[15]   For a concise exposition of this argument see Richard Swinburne, 'The Structure of the Soul', in: A. R. Peacocke, G. Gillett (eds.), *Persons and Personality*, pp. 33-54.

personhood. The practical historicism of the intellectual climate of the 20th century also maintains many historical approaches to the issue of personhood as intellectual options for today. The Hegelian notion, for instance, that the personal subject is truly actualized only in relation to the other so that particularity and identity are always relationally mediated, is therefore as much a feature in contemporary discussions as Kierkegaard's criticism of what he saw as the conflation of the Infinite and the finite in Hegel, which finds constructive expression in Kierkegaard's conception of the existential dialectics in which a finite personal subject as a self-relating relationship is involved.[16] The different philosophies dubbed as 'Personalism' also contribute to the context of current thinking on the nature of personhood: from Martin Buber's, Ferdinand Ebner's and Franz Rosenzweig's dialogical personalism[17] with its emphasis on the dialogical constitution of personhood in the dependence of the 'I' on the 'Thou' (which is sharply distinguished from the 'I' — 'It' relationship) to Emmanuel Mounier's and Denis de Rougemont's personalism where the primacy of the person before all material necessities and collective institutions is postulated as the basis for a comprehensive philosophy of society and culture.[18]

Thematically, many of the constitutive elements of philosophies of personalism overlap with emphases of the social psychology of G. H. Mead on the sociality of personal life according to which the 'Self' as the sum of the role-ascriptions of the social environment of persons has to be critically and constructively appropriated by the 'I' in order to make reciprocal social interaction possible.[19] Reflections on the formation and character of personal identity in modern psychological theories combine in many cases the seminal insights of this understanding of the social character of personal identity with modifications of the early views of the founding fathers of psychoanalysis that the conscious orientation of per-

[16] Cf. especially the first section in Kierkegaard's Sickness Unto Death (New York: 1962).

[17] F. Ebner's Das Wort und die geistigen Realitäten was published in 1922, the same year as F. Rosenzweig's Stern der Erlösung (The Star of Redemption, New York 1970, 1971), Buber's Ich und Du was published in 1924 (I and Thou, 2nd ed., New York: Charles Scribner's, 1953). The most extensive philosophical analysis of dialogical personalism is still: Michael Theunissen, Der Andere. Studien zur Sozialontologie der Gegenwart, 1965.

[18] Cf. D. de Rougemont's Penser avec les Mains and E. Mounier's Manifeste au Service du Personalisme, both first published in 1936.

[19] Cf. G. H. Mead, Mind, Self and Society (Chicago: University of Chicago Press, 1934).

sonal selves is shaped by the instincts, strivings and archetypical images of the subconsciousness, to some extent filtered by the normative precepts of an 'Ego-ideal' or the 'Super-Ego'. Here again are many points of contact to the analyses of the narrative reconstruction of personal identity through the selective appropriation of a subject's past and the structuring of its *Lebenswelt* which has fuelled the concentration of literary theory on the identity-determining role of narrative in literature.

Other conceptions have in different ways concentrated on the self-transcendence of human beings as the decisive element of human personhood. Self-transcendence as the capacity to go beyond the givenness of the natural in the instinctual equipment of humans and their relations to their biological environment, or to transcend the immediacy of the present, is variously described as human openness to the world, as the 'exocentricity' of human being and as openness to the future. The means of this transcending movement in its various aspects, from work and tools to language and culture, are in varying ways and in different orders of priority seen as constitutive for the actualization of what it means to be a human person.[20] Common to most of these views is the stress on the processual constitution of personhood. Being a person is seen in terms of being in a process of becoming a person in the personal actualization of human possibilities. This combination of the emphasis on self-transcendence and its implications for human freedom and the emphasis on the process of becoming in the actualization of personhood is a common denominator of many modern conceptions, although the character of self-transcendence and the nature of the process of becoming in which the potentialities of personal being are actualized are conceived in different, sometimes even incompatible ways.

The questions concerning the character of personhood are by no means exclusively the domain of abstract academic debates and pure scientific research. They lie at the heart of many burning public issues of our time from the ethics of genetic technology and medical research and practice to the debates about the character of legal responsibility and very practical issues of penal reform. The relevance of these questions is constantly underlined by the awareness of the human capacity for setting free depersonalising tendencies in their most destructive forms which characterize so much of twentieth century history. The contexts in which ques-

---

[20] *Cf.* Wolfhart Pannenberg's instructive account of the philosophical anthropology of Max Scheler, Helmuth Plessner and Arnold Gehlen in *Anthropology in Theological Perspective* (Edinburgh: T. & T. Clark, 1985), pp. 34-42.

tions about the character of personhood are raised vary from the global ecological crisis and the need for a reappraisal of the relationship of human persons to nature to the search for personal identity which motivates the demand for the various theories and techniques promising personal growth and self-fulfilment. Furthermore, it seems that some of the classical modern paradigms for defining personhood such as the conflict between political and economic liberalism and collectivist socialism become obsolete as determinants of debates about the nature of persons and its implications for individual freedom and social justice. The recent revolutionary changes in the countries of the former Eastern bloc seem to indicate not only the victory of political convictions based on the personal freedom of the individual over collectivist conceptions, but — at least on one level — also seem to point to the adoption by a large majority of the population in the former socialist countries of that most powerful of modern quasi-religions: consumerism. It is perhaps one of the ironies of our present historical situation that this practical orientation of life, where personal worth and freedom is primarily conceived by the degree of participation in the process of consumption, is enthusiastically welcomed by majorities in Eastern European countries when many in Western Europe and North America are beginning to be seriously concerned about the costs incurred in societies which adopt this value-orientation. What for one group appears as the highway to personal freedom, the other regards as one of the root causes of the 'depersonalization' of modern society.

II

Christian theology is intimately connected to many of the different notions of personhood which influence current debates about what it means to be a person and impinge on the development of our societies. There is much truth in Illingworth's claim that without Christianity the modern understanding of the significance of the person would have been impossible. Many of the conceptions we have mentioned in this brief survey have roots in biblical thought and Christian theology, in others Christian theology is confronted with its sometimes problematical side- and after-effects, while some were developed in conscious contrast to traditional conceptions of personal being in the Christian West. It cannot be denied that the Cartesian conception of the self as the *res cogitans*, understood in contrast to the *res extensa* of material existence — for all the criticism it receives today from Christian theologians — is deeply rooted in some strands of the Christian tradition and was devised, even if perhaps not primarily, for apologetic purposes. The idea of personal immortality, which forms part of its background, is already the product of the transformation of the Platonic idea of the immortality of the soul through the conviction of God's loving care for the individual person which will overcome even bodily death.[21] Augustine documents this transformation which entails the rejection of the idea of reincarnation as clearly as he provides evidence for the beginning of a strong dualist tradition of thinking on the person which owes more to the Neoplatonists than to the biblical writings. On the other hand, surprising though this may seem for those Christian theists who regard some form of dualism supporting the substantiality of an incorporeal soul as an integral element of a Christian view of reality, it is to be noted that a non-dualist conception of human nature has been vigorously supported by many theologians, and especially by biblical scholars. There is a far-ranging consensus of biblical exegetes that the view of what it means to be human in the biblical writings has a strong holistic emphasis, depicting human being as a unity of soul and body, mind and flesh.[22] Some theologians have gone to considerable lengths to reclaim some of the non-dualist emphases of materialism as genuine implications of such central Christian concepts as Creation, Incarnation, Resurrection and Ascension and see this holistic view of humanity as the common ground for reflection on human personhood.[23]

Hegel's conception of the mediation of personal particularity and identity through the other is grounded in a philosophical conceptualization of the religious notions of the doctrine of the Trinity, and the conflict between a Hegelian and a Kierkegaardian view of personal subjectivity can almost completely be construed as a battle over the implications of the doctrine of the Incarnation. Without the conceptual innovations of classical trinitarian theol-

---

[21] This is emphasized in Wolfhart Pannenberg's illuminating article 'Person und Subjekt', in *Grundfragen systematischer Theologie II* (Göttingen: Vandenhoeck & Ruprecht 1980), pp. 80-95, esp. pp. 81ff.

[22] A classic early and much quoted statement of this view can be found in H. Wheeler Robinson, *The Christian Experience of the Holy Spirit*, 1928 (London and Glasgow: Collins Fontana 1962), p. 28: 'Over against the Greek idea of an immortal soul temporarily inhabiting an earthly body, the Hebrew psychology gives us not an incarnated soul, but an animated body, as its characteristic doctrine of resurrection clearly shows, and this doctrine has proved able to maintain itself in its Pauline transformation, as the basis of the hope for the future.'

[23] An instructive example is Adrian Thatcher's 'Christian Theism and the Concept of a Person', in: A. R. Peacocke, G. Gillett (eds.), *Persons and Personality*, pp. 180-190.

ogy concerning the character of personhood and relation in the divine being, their conflict could not have taken this specific form. The indebtedness of personalist philosophies to biblical traditions and the conception of personhood in Jewish (Buber and Rosenzweig) and Christian mysticism (Ebner) or to Christian metaphysics (Mounier and de Rougemont) is part of their philosophical programme. And even where psychoanalytical reflection of personhood did not build constructively on the rich imagery of religion (Jung), but was critically perceived under the question of 'the future of an illusion' (Freud), Christian understandings of the person nevertheless provided the contrasting backdrop of many psychoanalytical contributions to the understanding of personhood.

The ambiguity which in some cases characterizes appropriations of elements of Christian traditions in modern conceptions of what it means to be a human person is especially evident in the use made of the notion of self-transcendence as one of the determinative elements of human personhood. On the one hand, theologians have argued that theology should reappropriate such modern conceptions since they are expressions of the eschatological destiny of human persons and their relationship to the transcendent personhood of God. On the other hand, it has been one of the standard elements of modern critiques of religion ever since Feuerbach that notions of a transcendent divine being are nothing but expressions of the self-transcendence of humanity in which humans do not relate to God, but to their own not yet actualized potentialities.

In reflecting on the nature of personhood in the context of the rich variety of contemporary conceptions, Christian theology does not encounter completely alien understandings of origins foreign to Christian traditions. Rather, Christian theology is confronted with many of the shadows of its own past, some in the guise of non-theological conceptuality, others with a decidedly anti-theological bias. There is no clear contrast between *the* Christian concept of the person and a number of non-Christian or secular accounts. In view of the theological origins of many of the secular conceptions, there is no one clearly defined Christian understanding of personhood which is to be contrasted with clearly defined secular notions. In attempting to present a Christian theological understanding of personhood Christian theology is therefore not only challenged to clarify what is *distinctively theological* in its accounts of personhood, but is also confronted with the task of finding criteria for what is *authentically Christian* in theological concepts of the person. And this task is to be carried out equally with regard to the many conceptions of personhood in Christian traditions as well as with regard to its side- and after-effects in many modern notions. This emphasizes the need for a theological perspective from which theological proposals about the distinctively theological and the authentically Christian in the understanding of the personal can be made and assessed.

In this connection the revival of trinitarian theology in many Christian theological circles in the last decade is of considerable significance.[24] This resurgence of trinitarian theological reflection is motivated by the conviction that Christian faith is irreducibly trinitarian in character and that a distinctively theological and authentically Christian perspective from which theology can engage in dialogue with the rich diversity of non-Christian and secular views of reality is therefore necessarily trinitarian. The theologians who have argued for this shift to trinitarian thought come from a variety of denominational traditions and theological schools. The ecumenical dialogue of the last decades, which has led to an exchange between Western and Eastern theologies unknown since the end of the patristic era, would certainly seem to be one contributing factor to the new trinitarian awareness in theology. The reasons for the new trinitarian orientation are as diverse as the theological and ecclesial backgrounds of the theologians advocating it. Dissatisfaction with the theological possibilities non-personal, unitarian or unipersonalist conceptions of God leave open for a reasoned account of the central claims of Christian faith about the person of Christ and his saving work is among the reasons for the renewed interest in trinitarian theology, supported by disappointment with the inability of many versions of Christian theism, conceived in terms of a metaphysics of substance or a philosophy of subjectivity, to do justice to the relational 'logic' of such central Christian statements as 'God is Love'. The positive motivations and expectations concerned with the revival of trinitarian thought range from the revitalisation of Christian orthodoxy and the validation of the conceptual scheme of Christian metaphysics to the propagation of forms of 'social personalism' or 'personal socialism'.[25]

---

[24] A clear indication of this renaissance of trinitarian theology is the Report of the BCC Study Commission on Trinitarian Doctrine Today *The Forgotten Trinity* (London: The British Council of Churches, 1989). Cf. also: Ronald J. Feenstra, Cornelius Plantinga Jr. (eds.), *Trinity, Incarnation and Atonement. Philosophical and Theological Essays.* Library of Religious Philosophy, Vol. I (Notre Dame: University of Notre Dame Press, 1989), especially pp. 3-13.

[25] Cf. J. Moltmann, *The Trinity and the Kingdom*, trans. Margaret Kohl (London: SCM Press, 1981), pp. 7 and 199.

In spite of the different motivations for this trinitarian turn in many strands of recent theology and the diverse expectations invested in it, there is nevertheless a considerable consensus concerning the status and significance of the doctrine of the Trinity. The doctrine of the Trinity is not regarded as one doctrine among others in the doctrinal scheme of Christian dogmatics, so that changes in its conception would have only limited implications for the systematic exposition of Christian faith. On the contrary, it is seen as determining the systematic structure of Christian dogmatics and its content in all its parts.[26] A trinitarian approach radically affects the exposition of who is the God in whom Christians believe, and the presentation of what can be asserted about God's being and the God-world relationship. Therefore the doctrine of the Trinity determines what can theologically be said about God as well as what can be stated about the world and humankind. Only because of this comprehensive status can trinitarian theology constitute a Christian theological perspective on reality. The trinitarian turn in theology therefore has implication for the whole of Christian dogmatics in all its parts.

A second point is closely connected with this. The displacement of the doctrine of the Trinity to an appendix of the doctrine of the one God and his attributes and the relegation of trinitarian language to the sphere of speculation or worship, which Karl Rahner has forcefully criticized,[27] is — at least to a significant extent — one of the consequences of the conception of this doctrine in the Augustinian tradition. This approach starts from the unity of the divine essence and not from the particularity of the trinitarian persons, expounds the Trinity through analogies of mental acts of an individual self-consciousness, and conceives of the unity of divine agency — apart from the Incarnation — in terms of the uniformity of divine action, as expressed in the famous tag *opera trinitatis ad extra sunt indivisa*.[28] Overcoming the virtual dis-

---

[26] For this understanding of the doctrine of the Trinity as 'theologische Strukturtheorie' cf. my article 'Die Rede vom Handeln Gottes im christlichen Glauben. Beiträge zu einem systematisch-theologischen Rekonstruktionsversuch', in: W. Härle/R. Preul (eds.), *Vom Handeln Gottes*. Marburger Jahrbuch Theologie I (Marburg: N. G. Elwert Verlag, 1987), pp. 56-81, esp. pp. 78ff.

[27] Cf. Karl Rahner, *The Trinity*, trans. Joseph Donceel (London: Burns & Oates, 1969).

[28] Cf. Robert Jenson's analysis in 'The Triune God', in: C. E. Braaten, R. W. Jenson, *Christian Dogmatics* (Fortress Press: Philadelphia, 1984), Vol. I, pp. 79-191, esp. 149ff.

placement of the doctrine of the Trinity therefore requires a departure from what for many centuries seemed like a minimal consensus of the mainstream of Western thought on the Trinity. If the doctrine of the Trinity is therefore to be seen as being not of marginal, but of central significance for Christian dogmatics the theological presuppositions which contributed to this marginalization have to be overcome, or must, at least, be modified.

A common element of modern trinitarian theology has therefore been a move away from what has somewhat misleadingly been called a psychological model of the Trinity to a social trinitarianism. This reorientation has been characterized by a constant rethinking of the seminal insights of the Cappadocian Fathers who approached the doctrine from the personal particularity of the *hypostaseis* of Father, Son and Spirit rather than from the undifferentiated generic essence of the Godhead and assessed their unity in terms of personal communion rather than essential sameness. In the tradition of Western thought Augustine's analogy of love as it was creatively redeveloped and conceptualized in the trinitarian theology of Richard of St Victor became the focus of new attempts to formulate trinitarian conceptions, rather than Augustine's account of the *vestigia trinitatis* in the mental acts of an individual consciousness.[29] With these conceptual changes the concept of the person acquired a new significance for trinitarian thought. In the Augustinian tradition primarily regarded as a problem, it now became a promise for the trinitarian reconstruction of theology[30].

These two developments form part of the specific background for the essays in this volume. If the new trinitarian approach to Christian doctrine is not only concerned with slight modifications in the doctrine of God, but has implications for the whole of Christian dogmatics, and if the concept of the person is a major element in these reconsiderations, then Illingworth's classic topic of the relationship of human and divine personality becomes a central focus for theological reflection. The perspective from which it is approached, has, however, changed significantly. The 'psychological model' is no longer the dominant one which constitutes the understanding of the concept of personality and which is then — as in Illingworth's case — modified and expanded through the 'social model'. Rather, reflection starts from the personal particularity of persons as it is constituted in their

---

[29] Cornelius Plantinga, Jr. 'Social Trinity and Tritheism', in *Trinity, Incarnation and Atonement*, pp. 21-47.

[30] *Cf.* Colin Gunton, *The Promise of Trinitarian Theology* (Edinburgh: T. & T. Clark, 1991).

personal relations in personal communion. The question is not primarily how reflection on human personality can offer grounds for the affirmation of divine personality, but rather how the insights concerning the character of divine personhood can be creatively applied to elucidate the understanding of human personhood. Some of the central questions which form the background of the reflections in most of these essays are therefore: What are the changes for the concept of personhood if it is no longer primarily understood in terms of individuality and substantiality, but on the basis of relational particularity and communion? What are the modifications that are necessitated in our conceptual framework of thinking about God and of reflection on humanity by the approach from a trinitarian concept of the person? What distinguishes and what unites divine and human personhood and how is their relationship to be conceived? However, both approaches, from human to divine personhood and from divine to human personhood, cannot be ultimately incompatible if it is the created destiny of human persons to be in the image of God and their eschatological promise to participate through the Spirit in the personal relationship of the Son to the Father. One of the central questions for the discussion in these essays is whether the trinitarian mode of reflection can contribute to a perspective for the consideration of what it means to be a person which is both distinctively theological and authentically Christian, and which can in this way contribute to a dialogue with other conceptions in Christian traditions and in the diversity of the intellectual climate of our times.

III

The first two papers raise many of the central philosophical and theological issues of the debate about personhood against a rich tapestry of reflection in the Eastern and Western traditions. Their systematic proposals form part of the backdrop of the following four essays where important aspects of the understanding of being a person are analyzed in the context of distinctive conceptions in the patristic and modern era. The last paper attempts to show how a conception of personhood can be systematically located in the framework of Christian Anthropology. All papers were originally presented and discussed in the weekly research seminars at the Research Institute of Systematic Theology at King's College, London and were revised for publication in the light of these discussions.

The first paper, 'On Being a Person' by John Zizioulas, Metropolitan of Pergamon, who as Visiting Professor at King's College took part in the seminars of the Research Institute, is devoted to the task of exploring the foundations of an ontology of personhood. This enterprise is, however, confronted with startling difficulties, since the claim for the absoluteness of particularity which John Zizioulas sees expressed in the question 'Who am I?' does not find much resonance in the history of ontological reflection in philosophy. In ancient Greek philosophy and in modern existentialist thinking, Professor Zizioulas argues, the particularity of the 'many' is always conceived against the backdrop of an ontologically primary 'one' which functions as the general horizon for the interpretation of the personal particularity of otherness.

In his reflections Zizioulas invites the reader to attempt a reversal of this perspective and to follow the view of the Hebrew Scriptures which gives priority to the particular by interpreting being in general as caused by God. The primacy of God and, implicitly, the ontological priority of particularity is, in his view, apophatically expressed in the statement 'I am that I am' where particularity fully coincides with constancy of being and articulation. The biblical emphasis on particularity which is one of the specific characteristics of the view of reality expressed in the Hebrew Scriptures is, in Zizioulas' view, taken up and developed in patristic theology, especially in the thought of the Cappadocians. It underlies the attempt at determining the general being of 'humanity' by pointing to its derivation from the particular being of Adam. However, this approach remains in itself insufficient as a foundation for the ontological priority of the particular. Determining the general being of humanity through its derivation from the particular being of Adam would require a constant relationship between Adam and the totality of humanity — a constancy of being which is impossible for a finite being. The conclusion Zizioulas draws with the Cappadocian Fathers is that in order to conceive of the ontological primacy of particular being, it is necessary to move from the anthropological to the theological plane.

It is in the Cappadocian doctrine of the Trinity that Professor Zizioulas finds the foundation for an ontology of personhood. It is to be seen in the relationship of Father, Son and Spirit as it is grounded in the particular being of the Father, the *fons et origo Trinitatis*. Here particular being is ontologically primary, i.e. not dependent on qualities borrowed from a prior general nature, and relational, i.e. grounded in a relationship which is constant and indissoluble. When we ascribe divinity to Father, Son and Spirit the particular beings of Father, Son and Spirit are bearers of the totality of nature, so that the relationship between the One and the Many need not be seen as one of contradiction. Zizioulas observes that this requires a transition from an ontology of substance to an ontology of love where love is understood as a relationship in which unique and absolute identity is created.

The question is, however, what this ontology of personhood, rooted in the personal communion of the Trinity, can offer for the understanding of the human person. For Zizioulas, the way in which the human striving for personhood finds fulfilment can only be expressed in a christological context. Following the lead of Chalcedon, Zizioulas asserts that Christ's personal identity is ontologically defined exclusively through the particular relationship of the Son to the Father. The natures only have being insofar as they are particularized in his person. The general qualities of the natures therefore have no independent existence apart from their personal particularisation in the *hypostasis* of the Son. They have being by being 'enhypostasized' so that the particular being of the person of the Son is ontologically primary to the general qualities of the natures.

Human persons can participate in this primacy of the personal by being included in the relationship of 'sonship' to the Father in Baptism, so that their identity is no longer defined in terms of the possession of general properties of created natures, but through the sacramental participation in the Father-Son-relationship. The ontological foundation of personhood as it is rooted in the personal communion of Father, Son and Spirit, christologically established for humanity in the hypostatic union and sacramentally mediated as inclusion in the uncreated Father-Son-relationship, cannot, however, according to Zizioulas, be fully realized in history as long as human beings remain dependent on nature. Its full realization remains a matter of hope in the eschatological transformation of the world.

While the argument of Professor Zizioulas' paper relies heavily on the insights and conceptual tools of Greek patristic thought, the next paper by Colin Gunton, Professor of Christian Doctrine at King's College, sets the question in a much wider context of the history of ideas. In his 'Trinity, Ontology and Anthropology: Towards a Renewal of the Doctrine of the *Imago Dei*' he distinguishes two central questions of theological anthropology: the ontological question concerning the being of the human and the comparative question of how the relationship of human beings to God and to other created beings should be described. The influence of the Cartesian understanding of the distinctively human in modern Western culture is, according to Professor Gunton, at least partly rooted in the fact that it provides one answer to both questions: humans reflect in their being the dual structure of the universe as matter and divine idea, and it is human reason which relates human being to the being of God and distinguishes it sharply from all other forms of created existence. This Cartesian conception points to two problematical aspects of anthropological thought in Western theological tradition. With regard to its method it is to a large extent dependent on the strategies of natural theology to proceed by speculative comparison and contrast from creation to God; with regard to its content it reveals a tendency to overstress the inner dimension of the person and to conceive what it means to be human exclusively in terms of rationality and consciousness, so tending to neglect the relationality and embodiedness of human personal existence. Both tendencies are in Colin Gunton's view connected with the Augustinian heritage of the Western intellectual tradition where this view is intricately related to a conception of the doctrine of the Trinity which is essentially conceived in terms of the self-relatedness of mental acts in the individual person. The upshot of this is that philosophical preconceptions seem to foreclose the constructive possibilities of theological anthropology, especially if it is shaped by the comparative methods of natural theology.

Professor Gunton does not attempt to resolve these difficulties by resorting to a theological approach that roundly condemns the use of philosophical categories as indicating the suspect influence of natural theology and whose constructive proposals might come close to the 'positivism of revelation' which Bonhoeffer suspected in Barth's theology. Rather, he attempts to approach the question indirectly by analyzing the interplay between cosmological and anthropological conceptions. From this interpretative perspective the dualist tendencies of anthropological thought in the Greek tradition seem to be intricately connected to the dualist structure of Greek cosmology, both in its mythological and in its philosophical form. Gunton is, however, not content to contrast these dualistic thought forms to the unitary approach which can be found in the Hebrew tradition and leads to a positive appreciation of matter and embodiment. Instead he follows Coleridge's typology of three world-views in his *On the Prometheus of Aeschylus*, where he compares the Phoenician world-view with its virtual identification of cosmogony and theogony and the dualist Greek view of reality with the Hebrew world-view. Gunton goes from Coleridge's discussion of the Hebrew world-view with its emphasis on the self-sufficient immutable creator to Coleridge's constructive development of the idea of God. Here Coleridge's perspective is defined by his view of the Trinity as the 'Idea Idearum, the one substrative truth which is the form, manner and involvement of all truths', the 'transcendental of transcendentals' in Gunton's conceptuality. From this vantage-point the concept of the person receives a central place in Coleridge's conceptual scheme, rooted in the idea of personeity which, in turn, is grounded in Coleridge's explication of the Trinity in terms of the perfect will. For Gunton, the fundamental intuition of Coleridge's conception is that 'relatedness' and 'space' have to be combined for an adequate understanding of the human person: both in relation to God and in the relations between finite persons, 'space' is required as the scope for the exercise of personal freedom. This insight then provides the criteria for the assessment of the Phoenician and the Greek views of reality where relation or space to be free seem to be either denied or misplaced.

Professor Gunton's own theological proposal for the understanding of the relationship between Trinity, ontology and the human person takes up Coleridge's insistence on the Trinity as the idea which defines the perspective from which this relationship is to be developed, but he differs from Coleridge in the conceptual description of the content of this idea. Instead of concentrating on the concepts of personeity and will, Gunton sees the trinitarian being of God more adequately expressed in terms of persons in communion who give to and receive from the other their particular identity. It is in this way that personal space is created: the freedom to be in relation to the other. This conception of God shapes for Colin Gunton the cosmological view of the world in Christian theology. As God's creation and dependent on being given space to be, it is characterized by otherness from God which is the world's freedom not to be God. But in this otherness it also 'echoes' the being of the creator, by existing as a dynamic relationship of being.

This understanding of createdness is, however, not yet sufficient to give a theological account of what it means to be in the image of God. Rather, it points, in Professor Gunton's view, to the inability of the non-human to realize its destiny apart from human persons — a view powerfully expressed in Paul's metaphor of the yearning of creation for the revelation of the children of God. Contrasting his conception of the image of God with views which locate it in human stewardship for creation or see it with Karl Barth in the male-female relationship, Gunton interprets the fundamental content of the *imago Dei* in being human as persons in relation, to be personally constituted in freedom and particularity, in otherness and relation. The human person is thus constituted as the image of God in relation to the trinitarian God by being conformed to the person of Christ in the Spirit and in relation to other created beings in the personal communion with other persons and in responsible stewardship for the cosmos. In this conception it becomes not only possible, Professor Gunton claims, to overcome the dualist implications of important strands of Western anthropology, because relations are relations of the whole person, body, soul and reason. It also opens up a way of answering the fundamental ontological and comparative questions of anthropology. Ontologically personhood becomes the chief category for determining the distinctive ontological status of the human and this determines the comparative and only relative difference of human beings from the non-personal creation as the task of responsible stewardship.

IV

Both these essays, which introduce the doctrine of the Trinity as the theological foundation for reflection on persons — divine and human — and approach the question of what is distinctive for the person from the perspective of free personal relations raise a number of questions. How can this new paradigm for reflection on the personal be related to the traditional emphasis on the dimension of consciousness, reflection and rationality as distinctive, at least, for the human person in the history of Western thought? Is it possible to integrate these insights that were developed in this framework into the new perspective which is determined by the priority it gives to personal relations? Or will the two conceptions always remain alternatives between which one has to choose? Professor Zizioulas as well as Professor Gunton point to the significance of Christology for any theological understanding of the person. For John Zizioulas the person of Christ as it is constituted in the relationship between Father and Son is the point where the primacy of the particular is disclosed to human understanding, and it is the ground for the eschatological realization of the human striving for personal identity. For Colin Gunton conformity with the person of Christ is the actuality of being in the image of God. The question which is raised by these approaches is whether it is generally true that the person of Christ should be regarded in theology as the paradigm for what it means to be human. If this is considered as a viable theological proposal, what are its implications for Christology and especially for the understanding of the humanity of Christ? This, of course, leads to further questions: if Christ becomes the paradigm for the truly human how can we account for the human condition as a fallen condition and how can the alienation of humanity from God be overcome? It is not only that any thesis asserting the necessity of a christological approach to the issues of anthropology immediately involve us in hamartiological and soteriological reflections.

These considerations are also of primary importance for describing the dynamic transformation that is involved in the realization of human personhood. It is in the context of the transformation from bondage to sin to the glorious freedom of the children of God that the relationship between the ground of human personhood and its destiny has to be theologically determined. The theological groundwork for reflection on the concept of the person is, however, not only validated by demonstrating its presuppositions and implications in other related doctrines, it also has to be shown as an adequate way of describing the reality of persons in the variety of contexts in which persons act and interact with one another and with non-personal being. Is a conception of personhood based on the trinitarian perspective of Christian faith able to provide an adequate framework for reflection on persons in the variety of concrete situations in which persons are involved?

These are some of the questions which are discussed in the next four essays in this collection. However, these issues are not only approached as systematic problems, they are also taken up in the context in which they present themselves in the thought of thinkers who made a significant contribution to reflection on personhood in the history of Christian thought. Dr Brian Horne, Lecturer in Christian Doctrine at King's College, starts his essay on 'Person as Confession: Augustine of Hippo' by referring to that period in the history of British theology when the concept of the person conceived in terms of personality was regarded as the centre from which a modern restatement of Christian beliefs should be developed. For R. J. Illingworth, perhaps the most original exponent of this school of thought at the turn of the nineteenth to the twentieth century, this concept of personality was decisively shaped by the intellectual traditions which are summarized in the names of Augustine, Luther and Kant. Dr Horne follows Illingworth's exposition of Augustine's thought which is centred not so much on his treatment of divine personhood in *De Trinitate*, but on its anthropological treatment in the *Confessions*. There the distinctively human is described not primarily in terms of reason, but as an explication of the tripartite structure of human consciousness where the interrelationship of existence, consciousness and will is seen as the highway for the discovery of personal identity. Dr Horne notes in passing that for Illingworth the self-reflective structure of human consciousness determines the approach to divine personality by means of analogy, rather than the tri-personal being of God which becomes accessible to us through God's self-communication in the divine economy.

Turning to the analysis of the *Confessions* Dr Horne follows suggestions for their interpretation made by Rebecca West who compared Augustine's work to Proust's *A la Recherche du Temps Perdu*, and thus indicated that the structure of the work disclosed a different aim than the exhortative, perhaps even rather moralistic intention, which Augustine himself declared. For Dr Horne this purpose is the definition of personal identity through recollection of the past which ascribes meaning to the changing scenes of life by giving it a selective narrative form. The narrative itself becomes, as Dr Horne points out by means of a comparison with Proust's masterpiece, the creation and comprehensive reconstruction of personal identity. This becomes possible through the power of memory which retains the past and thus provides the material for the narrative description of identity through the representation of a life-story. Although Augustine anticipated in this way, as Brian Horne emphasizes, many formative insights of modern psychoanalysis, these considerations are for him by no means restricted to a purely anthropological realm. Their theological significance becomes apparent from the way in which Augustine's theory of memory functions as the transition from anthropological to theological reflections in the *Confessions*, which are consequently centred on the investigation of the relationship of creativity and time. Furthermore, Dr Horne claims, it is the anthropology of the *Confessions* which provides the material for Augustine's psychological exposition of the *vestigia Trinitatis* in *De Trinitate*. Dr Horne's essay concludes with the question whether the different approach to the understanding of time — cosmological in the case of Gregory of Nyssa, for instance, psychological in Augustine's — is one issue which lies at the heart of the contrast of Eastern and Western approaches to central theological issues including the nature of personhood and the conception of the Trinity.

The paper 'Christ's Humanity and Ours: John Owen' by Dr Alan Spence, who completed his doctorate at King's on the Christology of the Puritan divine John Owen in 1989 and now teaches theology in his native Zimbabwe, explores the possibilities of regarding the person of Christ rather than the first human creatures in the *status integritatis* before the Fall as the paradigm of the truly human. According to Alan Spence, however, this approach has, in spite of its theological attraction, a number of difficulties with respect to its christological presuppositions. This is shown in the well-known dilemma: traditional Christologies which strongly affirm the divine sonship of Christ sometimes seem to run the risk of not being able to do full justice to the humanity of Christ as it is depicted in the Gospel narratives; modern Christologies which take the humanity of Christ as their starting-point often have difficulties in affirming Christ's divine sonship as it is expressed in the central statements of Christian faith.

In order to resolve this dilemma and to clarify the christological presuppositions of a theological anthropology which sees Christ as the paradigm of what it means to be human, Dr Spence introduces John Owen's Christology as an example of a conception which combines an incarnational doctrine of the Person of Christ with the emphasis on his humanity as the prototype of the human personhood of the believer. This is achieved through a christological theory which states that though the eternal Son assumed human nature into personal union with himself, the Word of God does not act directly and immediately on the human nature, but only through the Holy Spirit whose mode of operation leaves Christ's human nature intact so that it can serve as the paradigm of our humanity. Owen argues that the divine image in human beings, lost in the Fall, is first renewed in Christ's human nature so that Christ becomes the prototype of a new humanity where the divine image is restored. Owen interprets the conformity with Christ as being effected by the agency of the Holy Spirit, just as the Holy Spirit creates in the humanity of Christ the divine image by energizing, sanctifying and perfecting it. The operation of the Holy Spirit is in this way seen as constitutive both for the renewal of the divine image in Christ and for the transformation of the Christian life into conformity with Christ and thus into the likeness of the divine image.

In arguing for a christological approach which takes up the insights of Owen's conception, Dr Spence offers a number of related arguments. First of all, he shows that christological conceptions which follow the classical pattern established by Athanasius and see the Word of God as the governing principle of the humanity of Christ, at least run the risk of developing this approach to an Apollinarian conclusion: that the Word of God replaces the intellectual active functions of the human nature in the life of Christ. Against this tendency Alan Spence invokes the corrective of the Chalcedonian Definition which is summarized in the formula that in the hypostatic union 'the characteristic property of each nature [is] being preserved' which Owen, building on the conceptuality of Leo's *Tome*, developed into the theory that Christ's human nature is 'autokineton', a self-determining spiritual principle. This view of the humanity of Christ is presupposed in Owen's soteriological theory that in his office as priest Christ offers himself as a sacrifice to God the Father, which in Owen's interpretation refers to the giving up of his human nature and so undergoing the dereliction of Gethsemane and the death of Calvary. In this redemptive process Christ's humanity is to be seen as fully human, actively operating according to its own principles energized through the Holy Spirit and not as directly determined by the Word of God. Thirdly, Dr Spence contrasts Owen's conception with Barth's understanding of divine self-revelation. Barth's thesis that God is revealed by God through God might, he asserts, lead in Christology to the assumption of a strict discontinuity between the Word of God and the historical Jesus (which seems to be one of the characteristics of the Christology of the early Barth), whereas Owen's view that Christ revealed the will of the Father in and by his human nature allows us to retain the full historical reality of the Christ-event without reducing its theological significance. One of the implications of this view is — as Dr Spence points out — that the self-consciousness of Jesus should not be seen as discontinuous in character with our own self-understanding. While its distinctive content is the unique relationship of the Son to God the Father, this content is disclosed to Jesus and gradually develops in a manner which is continuous with our experience of sanctification as it is enabled, supported and brought to its truth by the Holy Spirit.

Dr Spence's paper does not only show how the trinitarian approach to the issues raised by the relationship between divine and human personhood makes possible the rediscovery and re-appraisal of theological conceptions such as Owen's which do not belong to the received canon of the history of doctrinal theology; it furthermore demonstrates the systematic interrelationship between the doctrines of Christian anthropology, Christology and the doctrine of the Trinity. If the personhood of Christ is to be seen as the paradigm of what it means to be truly human, his humanity cannot be seen as in any sense curtailed or restricted to the abstract possession of a human nature by the divine Word. If this emphasis on the complete active humanity of Christ is to be integrated into an incarnational Christology, this approach must be part of a genuinely trinitarian framework for Christology, where the Holy Spirit is seen as the one who enables, supports and perfects the relationship of the incarnate Son to the Father and draws believers by grace into this union. One of the interesting results of such an approach is that this trinitarian understanding of the Incarnation not only provides a basis for seeing Christ's humanity as the paradigm of true humanity, but requires also the recognition of the human historical reality of the human life of the earthly Jesus. Here Owen anticipates, as Dr Spence shows, one of the major concerns of modern Christology without being led into the antinomies between the historical and the theological which have haunted so many modern discussions of Christology.

The next essay 'Strange News from Another Star: An Anthropological Insight from Edward Irving' by Dr Graham McFarlane, who completed his doctorate on Irving at King's in 1990 and is now a Lecturer at the London Bible College, goes in many ways over similar ground to that of the previous essay. Irving shared with Owen the strong trinitarian emphasis of his theology, the biblical orientation of his thought and a lively awareness of the significance of the Holy Spirit in Christian theology. Some of these similarities of approach may be due to their shared heritage in Calvinist theology. But whereas Owen's thought is, in spite of the turbulent times in which he lived, characterized by the metaphysical confidence of a technical theology which is sure of its ground and direction, Irving's thought is as much as his life characterized by the greater disquiet of post-Enlightenment thought, where the foundations of Christian theology had to be reconstructed in a way convincing to its age. The awareness of the dynamics of history, of the insecurity of the place of humankind in the cosmos, the urgency of the theodicy question in the face of the fallenness of the human condition, experienced both individually and socially, gives Irving's theologizing a different tone from Owen's reflections.

Dr McFarlane presents Irving's anthropological considerations against the background of his christological and soteriological, especially hamartiological, thought. The central metaphor of the *imago Dei* is therefore not simply expounded in terms of a substantial distinction of humanity, but is developed as the focus of a multifaceted network of relations. The purpose of creating human beings is that they can exist in a relationship of worship to God which manifests God's glory. This is according to Irving always christologically mediated, so that humanity reflects the image of the Father in the eternal Son in being conformed to the incarnate Word of God and can do the will of the Father in constant dependence on the grace of God's Spirit. Irving's particular emphasis is, according to Dr McFarlane, to be found in his description of the operation of both the *imago Dei* and the *dominium terrae* in a conception centered on the notion of the will. In their free, willing response to the will of God which is an expression of divine freedom human beings attain their destiny to be in the image of God. Both the reflection of the freedom of the Son who is the image of the invisible Father and the exercise of dominion in creation is performed through the embodied human will which is therefore the decisive link between the Creator and the creatures.

For Irving the crucial point is not simply the mapping out of these relationships, but their dynamic enactment in the history of salvation. He therefore attempts to reconcile an archaeological interpretation of humanity which has its paradigm in the original righteousness of the first Adam before the Fall with a teleological interpretation focussed on Christ as the paradigm for the ultimate destiny of what it means to be human, in what Dr McFarlane describes as perfect beings, but as yet incomplete. Their form of existence is described as 'soul', the embodied connection of spirit and matter which, however, only has a capacity for, but has as yet no actual knowledge of God, Father, Son and Spirit. The relationship to the incarnate Son which is at the heart of the human destiny as the *imago Dei* is as yet unrealized. Adam is the type of Christ and creation incomplete without redemption.

As Graham McFarlane shows, this leads Irving to a sustained attempt to develop a fully-fledged theological notion of the Fall and the overcoming of its consequences in Christ. Here Irving's theological understanding of the destiny of humanity comes to full fruition. The state of human existence before the Fall is perfect, but incomplete, preparatory for the state which could only be achieved in relation to the incarnate Christ. Dr McFarlane distinguishes in Irving's treatment of the Fall a cosmological and an ontological perspective. According to the former it is necessary that the creature should fall in order to become aware of the distinction of created existence from the creator, to know the derived character of created goodness which has no capacity to maintain itself. Creation itself is not the end of God's work, but a creation united to God in the Spirit through the Son. Therefore the human creature had to fall to make way for the free relationship of obedience to God's will as disclosed in the Son. The Fall is for Irving the uncaused act of the free created will to be more than Adam, but nevertheless there is no divine culpability for the happening of the Fall. Dr McFarlane duly notes the pitfalls of this conception, but he also points to the dangers of distorting Irving's conception which arise when elements of Irving's conceptions are isolated from his comprehensive conception, centred on the purpose of God in Christ. This emphasis becomes evident when the Fall is seen from the ontological perspective. In order to be *imago Dei*, to choose the good on the basis of the awareness of good and evil, so that the ontological primacy of God the Son could be recognized in the acceptance of the atonement of sin wrought by the incarnate Son, the Fall is preparatory for the full achievement of the human destiny. This is closely connected to Irving's insistence, carefully expounded by Dr McFarlane, that the sacrifice of Christ is of a prior ontological order to creation, that it is to be located in the eternal holiness of the Godhead. Therefore the atonement is not only a temporary remedy consequent upon the Fall, but essentially rooted in the eternal being of God, Father, Son and Spirit. This is why the Fall does not take God unawares and why God is capable of dealing with sin so that redeemed humanity can be taken up into unity with the Father through the

Son in the Spirit. Eden is lost, so that the Kingdom can be gained.

Irving was a 'high risk theologian', and it can be argued that he ultimately became the victim of the expectations the adventurous mood of his theology raised in others. Nevertheless, Dr McFarlane succeeds in showing that Irving's anthropology is one of the first conceptions which reflects both the modern insistence on human personhood as being-in-relation and being-on-the way *and* the modern experience of estrangement, and is able to integrate them in the framework of a trinitarian conception of the divine economy. In this respect his thought can be a considerable inspiration for modern theology.

With the next paper, the last in this section, the Revd. John Aves' 'Persons in Relation: John Macmurray', we move to a quite different territory: the 'personalist' philosophy of John Macmurray which brings us very close to contemporary concerns about personhood. Macmurray was concerned with the 'crisis of the personal' in modernity which, according to John Aves' description, he saw expressed in two significant tendencies of modern society: the apotheosis of the state which leads to a functional view of personal life and the decline of (Christian) religion which had insisted on the ultimacy of personal values and whose decline will, in Macmurray's view, support both the depersonalizing tendencies in the apotheosis of the state and a manipulative style of political leadership and social interaction. Philosophy has, in Macmurray's eyes, by and large failed to counteract the tendencies towards depersonalization: by conceiving reality in terms of mathematical form or organic structure, and by starting from the notion of the self as an isolated thinker which for Macmurray leads to 'logical individualism'. He therefore suggested a change in philosophy's standpoint: from the predominance of the Cartesian *res cogitans* to the primacy of person in relation and from the perspective of theoretical reflection to the perspective of reason as exemplified in personal, intentional agency.

Macmurray reconstructs the constitution of the person, as John Aves shows, in an analysis of the mother-child relationship as the basic form of human existence which exhibits the mutuality of love as the fundamental motive pattern of personal relations. The relationship of love is closely related to fear (of not having one's needs met) and resentment (as a reaction against the refusal of the other to enter into a relationship). John Aves reconstructs how Macmurray develops from this basis a criteriology which is intended to cover our whole experience and explains the occurrence of contemplative 'idealist' attitudes and aggressive 'pragmatist' attitudes from unresolved conflicts in the primordial personal relationship of child and mother. This relationship is for Macmurray also the key to the understanding of religion as the universal, all-inclusive, personal basis of all aspects of culture where in the relationship to God as the Other communal life is integrated, attains stability in time and over against nature, and secures the capacity for free personal action. The understanding of God as the personal Other in relation to whom we have our personal being and freedom, and the understanding of the world as God's action function as strong safeguards in Macmurray's thought against a dualistic conception of ourselves and the world.

John Aves' analysis of Macmurray's conception leads to a number of critical questions which can help to determine to what extent and in what way Macmurray's conception can be appropriated in a theological understanding of divine and human personhood. From a theological perspective it is by no means clear whether the personal constitution of human being can be read off our experience of the way things go in the world. A conception which makes this assumption is in danger of reducing the experience of evil and sin to unresolved tensions in personal relationships (Macmurray's fear and hatred) and is theologically bound to pass by the central claim, as developed, for instance, in Owen's or Irving's conception, that the true nature of personhood is inextricably bound up with the significance of the life, death and resurrection of Jesus Christ. The central notions of Christian anthropology like original sin, atonement and the consummation of human destiny seem to refer to serious dimensions of the distortion of personal life and the need for their redemption which seem to be understated in Macmurray's account. Furthermore, Aves points out that there is a tendency in Macmurray's thought to contrast personal and impersonal relations in such a way that it becomes difficult to account for the highly differentiated social life in which we participate where many roles and relations seem to refer to an intermediate realm, the 'middle distance' of our relationships, which lacks the intimacy of Macmurray's paradigmatic personal relations and the objectifying tendencies of his description of impersonal relations. Aves shows that Christian theology does not necessarily have to embrace such a restrictive notion of personal relations, because it has resources for the understanding of the personal, such as dialectics of law and gospel or the eschatological tension of 'yet' and 'not yet' which could help to do justice to the factual differentiation of our communal and social life. Moreover, Aves refers to the understanding of the relational being of God in the communion of Father, Son and Spirit and the incarnational notions of the unity of human persons and their role as the priests of creation in the

Greek Fathers to indicate the possibilities of a constructive development of the theme of persons in relation which the tradition offers.

Aves is careful not to advocate a total rejection of Macmurray's analysis of the personal. It remains a valuable contribution to the understanding of the mutuality of personal relations and to the personal character of intentional action. However, Macmurray's example shows that Christian theology does not have to develop its understanding of what it means to be a person by 'baptizing' personalist philosophies, but has its own resources for a constructive account of personhood which can critically make use of the philosophical conceptions of its time.

V

The last paper in the collection, 'Human Being As Relational Being', is, like the first two papers, a systematic exploration. It is, however, not intended to present a detailed exposition of one particular aspect of the theme of this book, like the ontology of personhood or the doctrine of the *imago Dei*. Rather, it is an attempt to relate some of the issues discussed in this volume to the over-all conception of a Christian anthropology. Therefore it offers a series of theses which present a proposal for mapping out an approach and a systematic structure for the doctrinal project of a Christian theological understanding of what it means to be human.

The paper starts from the observation that the understanding of human being as relational being forms a common element in many contemporary approaches to anthropology. The distinctive perspective of Christian theological anthropology is, however, to be seen as expressed in the conviction that human being as relational being is rooted in the relationship of the triune God to humanity as it is disclosed in God's revelation in Christ through the Spirit. This does not mean that anthropology has to proceed 'from above'. Its appropriate starting-point, it is suggested, is Christian faith as the form of life where the relationship of the triune God to humanity is acknowledged as the foundation of human being as relational being. The perspective of faith is not only described as epistemologically determinative for a Christian view of what it means to be human, but is also conceived ontologically as the mode of being in which humans actualize their relational being in accordance with God's relationship to humanity. Because the relationship of faith has eschatological ultimacy (although the knowledge of faith remains distinct from the beatific vision of the *eschaton*), it can be characterized by Paul Tillich's concept of New Being which combines three dimensions: the relational being of faith is understood to be creatively new (since it is not a step in the natural evolution of the human species), it is described as new in the sense of the reconstitution of the created destiny of humanity and, thirdly, as new in the sense of being the fulfilment of the relationship between God and humanity.

The next theses attempt to sketch the relationship of this anthropological approach to central themes of soteriology and Christology. On this view, faith is soteriologically characterized by the overcoming of sin and its effects (conceived in terms of contradiction and dislocation) by the justifying grace of God. In this connection Luther's 'definition' that being truly human means to be justified by God (*hominem justificari fide*) is introduced. It is suggested that the anthropological implications of the understanding of justification presupposed here can be expressed in terms of the recreation of the human destiny to live in the image of God as the image of Christ. The influence of Reformation theology on the conception developed in this sketch is also apparent in the thesis that conformity with Christ in faith through the justification of the sinner is to be seen as the complete definition of the human person. The notion of conformity with Christ is further developed as participation through the gift of the Spirit in the relationship of the Son to the Father. It is suggested that the relationship between divine personhood and human personhood presupposed in this conception should be understood as an *analogia transcendentalis*: the tri-personal being of God is to be conceived as the condition for the possibility of personal human being as well as the condition for knowledge about the constitution of human personhood.

In Christian theology the relationship of human persons to God is seen as determinative for the whole network of relationships in which human being exists as relational being. In this sense it is argued that the social dimension of human personal being finds its personal and communal expression in the church as the witness to the recreation of humanity's created sociality as redeemed sociality. The relationship of human beings to nature, it is suggested, should, on this view, be interpreted in terms of responsible stewardship. The cultural activity of human beings, which shapes their social relationships and their relationship to nature, is furthermore characterized by the concept of co-creatorship, understood as the exercise of the finite and dependent creativity of human beings. The eschatological dynamic in which human being as relational being is actualized is proposed in the final thesis as the ultimate horizon for a theological conception of a Christian anthropology.

This essay points to two tasks which appear to be suggested by the reflections in this volume. First of all, if Christian theology is to engage in a fruitful dialogue with reflections on the personal in non-theological disciplines and in non-Christian views of reality, it seems necessary to establish a theological perspective which reflects the distinctiveness of Christian faith and its constitution. Secondly, and this is in many ways illustrated by all the contributions, it appears to be an important requirement for establishing such a theological perspective to consider how reflection on the relationship between concepts of divine and human personhood can be located within the doctrinal scheme of Christian faith and can in this way be related to other central doctrines of Christianity. Both tasks may be approached by quite different routes than those suggested in this essay, but they cannnot be evaded, if Christian theology remains committed to the task of presenting a coherent and plausible framework of Christian beliefs.

The essays in this volume cannot claim to offer an exhaustive systematic treatment of the relationship of divine and human personhood in all its aspects, and they are not intended as the presentation of a programmatic new approach to central issues of Christian theology. They are attempts at contributing to the ongoing conversation within Christian theology and of Christian theology with its intellectual context about the implications of the conviction of Christian faith that God is to be identified as Father, Son and Spirit and that it is the created destiny of human beings to attain personhood in relation to this triune God. In the context of such a conversation this volume too offers a series of explorations on the theological possibilities that are opened up, when the question of what it is to be a person — which is today hardly less relevant than it was in Illingworth's days — is approached not so much in terms of the relationship of *Personality*— *Human and Divine*, but from the perspective indicated by its title *Persons — Divine and Human.*

I

Theological Proposals

1. On Being a Person. Towards an Ontology of Personhood

John D. Zizioulas

Ontology is a word to which various meanings have been given, while for some people it indicates almost nothing at all. In this paper we take it to mean the area of philosophy (and theology) in which the question of *being* is raised more or less in the sense in which it was posed for the first time by ancient Greek philosophy[1] applied here to the specific problem of personal identity. What does it mean that someone *is* rather than *has* a person? It is all too often assumed that people 'have' personhood rather than 'being' persons, precisely because ontology is not operative enough in our thinking. Personhood in this case becomes a quality added, as it were, to being: you first (logically speaking) *are* and then *act* or *behave* as a person. This assumption rules out *a priori* an ontology of personhood and is not taken into account here. Instead, we operate with the view that the assertion of personal identity, the reduction of the question of 'Who am I?' to the simple form of the 'I am who I am', i.e. the claim of absolute metaphysical identity independent of qualities borrowed from other 'beings', is an assertion implied in the very question of personal identity. Personhood, in other words, has the claim of absolute being, that is, a metaphysical claim, built into it.

---

[1] This was more or less the sense in which the term *ontology* was employed for the first time in the seventeenth century by authors such as R. Goclenius (*Lexikon Philosophicum*, 1613) and, more explicitly, J. Glauberg (*Metaphysica de Ente*, 1656), who defines it as the part of philosophy which speculates on being *qua* being. The same definition is recovered and employed without change by Ch. Wolff (*Philosophia prima sive ontologia*, 1729, esp. §§ 1 and 2), who is responsible for the establishment of this term in philosophy. Kant in his *Critique of Pure Reason* (esp. ch. III) tried to give the term a different meaning, which however has not prevailed. Heidegger and the modern existentialist philosophers have also employed it with a different meaning in their attempt to take a critical view of classical philosophy, whereas authors such as E. Levinas in our time prefer not to attach to it the traditional metaphysical importance.

In the lines that follow we shall first pose the question that can be called 'personal' in the strictest sense, and try to elicit its ontological ingredients. We shall see how problematic a true ontology of personhood is, unless certain drastic revisions of philosophical thinking are introduced. These revisions will be considered as the presuppositions of an ontology of personhood. Against this background suggestions will be then offered for an attempt to work out an ontology of personhood with reference to the Christian doctrine of God.

I. The Personal Questions as an Ontological Question

1. Who am I? Who are you? Who is he/she? This question analysed in its basic components contains the following fundamental and indeed *constitutive* ingredients:

(a) The ingredient *Who*. 'Who' is a call for *definition* or 'description' of some kind. It is a call of and for *consciousness*, a desire for *articulation*, for knowledge in the most fundamental sense. Wanting to know *who* you are is a human question which seems at first sight to require a developed degree of consciousness, a capacity for reflection, and yet it is a primordial cry, stemming from the fact that man is faced with a *given* world, and thus forced into self-assertion always via comparison with other beings *already* existing.

(b) The ingredient 'am' or *to be*. This is a cry for security, for ground to be based on, for fixity. It is uttered in the face of two basic facts: the fact that we have not always been there, and the fact that things disappear, are not always there. To assert "being there", is to assert that you are overcoming not being there. It is a triumphalistic cry, or if you wish a doxological/eucharistic one, in the deepest sense of acknowledging being as a sort of victory over non-being. It is at the same time a cry of hidden fear in the face of non-being or the threat of death. The assertion of being is the recognition of the limitations or limits of being. It is a *kataphasis* implying an *apophasis*, the possibility or rather the actuality of a *beyond*, a movement of *transcendence*. Whether this 'beyond' leads to still other forms of being, or to pure and simple non-being, this is a matter of choosing between on the one hand, various forms of idealism, and on the other, extreme forms of existentialism. In either case the expression 'I *am*' cannot be understood apart from some kind of transcendence, from what might be called 'metaphysics'.

(c) The ingredient 'I' or 'You' or 'He/She'. This is a cry for *particularity*, for *otherness*. Other beings, besides the one spoken of under the question 'Who am I?', *are* — The second of our ingredients (the assertion of being) can be applied, therefore, to *many* beings, and so can the first one (the *who* ingredient), since it implies qualities borrowed from other beings. What this third ingredient implies is a sort of *uniqueness*, a claim of being in a unique and unrepeatable way. Many things 'are' but no one else is *me* (or you, etc.). This assertion is absolute: not simply because nothing else is 'me', but also because nothing else can *ever* be me.[2] Metaphysics in this case applies to 'me' as much as it does to 'am'. Hidden behind this is the cry for immortality, the desire not simply of the εἶναι but of the ἀεὶ εἶναι being for ever. The fact that being continues after the 'I' disappears or falls into non-being cannot be a consolation here. If we answer the question 'Who am I?' by simply saying 'I am a mortal being', we have removed the absoluteness from the ingredient 'I' and thus reduced it to something replaceable. This can be done, but immediately the problem of personal ontology will arise.

2. Personal ontology is an assertion of the metaphysics of particularity. It is the endeavour to raise the particular to the primacy and ultimacy which transcends the changing world of coming and going particularities; to attach fixity to the 'many' as if they were the 'one', i.e. absolute, unique and irreplaceable.

Ontology in the metaphysical sense of the transcendence of beings by being, i.e. in the sense of going beyond what passes away into what always and truly *is*, was the primary pre-occupation of ancient Greek thought. The flux in which things exist caused the Greek mind wonder and disturbance. You can never jump twice into the same river: how, then, can you say that this *particular* river *is*? 'Everything is in a flux', and yet things are true, and can be said to *be*. If this is not so then we are driven either to sophistry or to madness. Particularity does not extinguish being. The latter goes on for ever, while the particular beings disappear. True

---

[2] This rules out any ontologies implying transformations of particular beings, leading to emergence of *new* particular beings, as for example in the case of Platonic *metempsychosis*, or even the Aristotelian perpetuation of species through the emergence of particular beings. In both cases particularity ceases to be absolute in a metaphysical sense, since it is implied that a particular being is replaceable by another one. Contrasted with these particularities the personal "I" or "me" (or "he/she") involves the claim that *never* can there be an "I" other than this particular one to replace it in any way.

being, therefore, in the absolute, metaphysical sense cannot be attached to the particular except in so far as the latter is part of a *totality*. Ancient Greek thought in *all* its forms (Parmenidian, Heracletan, Platonic and Aristotelian), in spite of its variations on other aspects, agreed on one thing: particularity is not ontologically absolute; the many are always ontologically derivative, not causative.[3]

This ontology of the classical Greeks made a personal ontology impossible, as the third of the above mentioned ingredients had to be somehow sacrificed. The truth of any particular thing was removed from its particularity and placed on the level of a universal form in which the particular participated: the thing itself passes away but its form *shared by more than one particular thing* survives. The survival of Man was also subjected to the same principle. The Platonic soul of a human being, far from safeguarding the survival of the particular eternally, could be reincarnated in other beings, even in animals.[4] And Aristotle's concern with the particular did not lead to the survival of the concrete being for ever, except in the form of its species. The *οἷον* passes away; what survives is the *οἷον αὐτό*[5]

Thus Aristotelian ontology operated with the first two of our three ingredients, but not with the third one. The 'who' question was answered with the help of categories taken from something general, not from the particular thing itself (the 'I'). *οἷον αὐτό*— not the *αὐτό* is the answer to the question of the 'who'. But the *οἷον αὐτό* comprises qualities shared by other beings besides the *αὐτό* (the 'I') — hence the *αὐτό* cannot be ontologically ultimate. Participation in being is a condition for the particular's being as much for

---

[3]   Plato's words in the *Laws* (X, 903 c-d) are revealing: 'But thou failest to perceive that all partial generation is for the sake of the whole in order that for the life of the whole blissful existence may be secured. For it (the whole) is not brought into being for thy sake, but thou (the particular) art for its sake'. Neoplatonism, by attaching ontological priority and ultimacy to the 'one' and by regarding the 'many' as a sort of deterioration or 'fall' of being, as a tendency towards 'non-being', confirms the fact that classical Greek thought was basically and consistently monistic in its ontology, as is rightly remarked by C. J. de Vogel, *Philosophia* I, *Studies in Greek Philosophy*, pp. 397-416.

[4]   See Plato, *Timaeus* 41d-42e, in combination with *Phaedo* 249B, *Repub.* 618A etc.

[5]   See Aristotle's *De anima* 2, 4.415A, 28-67. Cf. E. Rohde, *Psyche*, 1925, p. 511, and H. A. Wolfson 'Immorality and Resurrection in the Philosophy of the Church Fathers', in K. Stendahl (ed.), *Immortality and Resurrection*, 1965, pp. 54-96.

Aristotle as it is for his master Plato. No ancient Greek managed to escape from this. The consequences on the existential level were inevitable. Classical tragedy enslaved its heroes — human *and* divine — in the destiny of natural or moral order and rationality. Man exists for the world, not the world for Man.

The inability of Greek thought to create a personal ontology is not due to a weakness or incapacity of Greek philosophy as *philosophy*. None in the history of philosophy has so far managed to work out a consistent ontology of personhood in the sense of incorporating the third of our three ingredients into the other two. The reason for this is both logical and existential. Logically, the particular is conceivable and can be spoken of only with the help of categories applicable to more than one thing. Such a category is *οὐσία* itself which accounts at the same time for the being of the particular and of what transcends it, hence Aristotle's oscillating between first and second substance, brought out so well by D. M. Mackinnon.[6] Existentially, on the other hand, death conditions the particular being so radically that only by joining being with death in a Heideggerian 'panoramic' view of existence[7] can we give to the 'how' of things a primary ontological role, thus securing for the particular a place in ontology. But this panoramic view of being presupposes still a *horizon* in which the particulars emerge, as is exactly the case in Heidegger's philosophy, and this 'horizon' is a unifying principle conditioning the 'many' and hence prior to them. Otherness cannot acquire ontological primacy as long as one begins with the world as it is, as did the ancient Greeks and as all philosophy does, if it wishes to be pure philosophy. The observation of the world cannot lead to an ontology of the person, because the person as an ontological category cannot be extrapolated from experience.[8]

II. Presuppositions for an Ontology of Personhood

1. In order to give to the particular an ontological ultimacy or priority it is necessary to *presuppose* that being is *caused* and

---

[6] D. M. Mackinnon, 'Substance in Christology — a Cross-bench view', in S. W. Sykes and J. P. Clayton (eds.), *Christ, Faith and History. Cambridge Studies in Christology*, 1972, pp. 279-300.

[7] See the critique of Heidegger by E. Levinas, *Totalité et Infinie. Essai sur l'Exteriorité*, 1974⁴, p. 15.

[8] More about this in our 'Human Capacity and Human Incapacity. A Theological Exploration of Personhood', in *The Scottish Journal of Theology*, 28 (1975) 401-448, esp. pp. 420f.

cannot be posited as an axiomatic of self-explicable principle. This causation must be absolute and primary in ontology, not secondary. Ancient Greek philosophy knew of causation, but it always posited it *within* the framework of being. Everything is caused by something else but the world as a whole is not caused *radically*, i.e. in the absolute ontological sense, by anything else. Plato's creator is an artist and an organizer of pre-existing being, and Aristotle's *nous* is the First Mover causing the world to move always *from within* and on the basis of an eternal ὕλη. The world is eternal; it is not ontologically caused. And so the particular is never the ontologically primary cause of being. This leads to necessity in ontology.[9] Being is not a gift but a datum to be reckoned with by the particular beings.

Biblical thought posited a different view of being. It is rightly said that Hebrew thought has no ontology to offer. For the Bible being is caused in a radical way by *someone* — a particular being. There is no attempt in the Bible to describe this 'someone' in terms of being, for this would lead to associating Him with the world and thus depriving Him of the capacity of cause in the absolute sense. At some point in the Bible He is described as ὁ ὤν rather in order to indicate in an apophatic manner that he is not to be described in any ontological way. Nevertheless in terms of our initial question in this paper the 'I am that I am' of the Bible offers an illustration of an assertion in which the particular (the third ingredient) coincides fully with the other two, the 'who' and the 'am'. We thus have a step towards an ontology of personhood.

This principle of personal causation of being means that particularity is to be understood as causative and not derivative in ontology. To illustrate this we may turn to Patristic thought which tried to apply this principle, stemming from the Bible, to ontology. Two examples can be significant for this purpose.

First the question of human being. What is it that causes particular human beings to *be*? Greek philosophy at the time of the Fathers was offering the choice between a Platonic οὐσία ὑπερκειμένη and an Aristotelian οὐσία ὑποκειμένη. In other words, the particular human beings *are* in so far as they participate either in the ideal 'Man' or in the 'nature' of humanity, its species. The particular is caused by the general.

To these two choices Patristic thought added a third one which it borrowed from the Bible. What causes the particular human beings to *be* is *Adam*,[10] i.e. *a particular being*. This way of thinking

---

[9]   For an attachment of the idea of being to that of necessity see E. Gilson, *L'esprit de la philosophie médiévale*, 1932, pp. 45-66.
[10] See note 12 below.

would create immense difficulties to Greek philosophy — or perhaps philosophy as a whole? At this point Biblical thought introduced a paradox quite unknown to Greek or, for that matter, to our Western way of thinking too. This paradox is known, ever since the British biblical scholar R. Wheeler Robinson coined the phrase, as *corporate personality*.[11] According to it, Semitic thought could move naturally from the 'one' to the 'many' and *vice versa*, by including in a particular being a unity of many, and by referring to a group of beings as one particular being. The examples from the Old Testament (as well as from the New) are numerous. It is noteworthy that they all refer to *human* beings — not to things or animals. In this sense ontology operates with the view that the fixed point of reference, the ground of being that offers security and truth, is a particular person and not a general idea or nature.

The second example is to be found in the Patristic doctrine of God. Here we must specify the term 'Patristic' to include mainly the Cappadocian Fathers. For before them the question of God's being, i.e. divine ontology, was not raised as an issue *in itself* (not in relation to the world, as was the case even still with St Athanasius, while after them with Augustine things took an altogether different direction in ontology). What is it that causes divine being to *be* and to be *particular beings*? The analogy of Adam which was applied to the human being, and not the οὐσία (ὑπερκειμέη or ὑποκεινένη) was applied also to this question.

The discussion of this matter is to be found in a very explicit form in the correspondence between St Basil and Apollinaris.[12] Basil asks Apollinaris to explain to him how one could avoid assuming "a substance lying above" (οὐσία ὑπερκειμένη) — a reference to Platonism — or a "substance lying underneath" (οὐσία ὑποκειμένη) — a probable allusion to Aristotelianism — in dealing with God, and particularly with the relationship between the

---

11 H. Wheeler-Robinson, *The Hebrew Conception of Corporate Personality*, 1936, pp. 49ff. Cf. A. R. Johnson, *The One and the Many in the Israelite Conception of God*, 1942; J. de Fraine, *Adam et son lignage: Etudes sur la "personalité corporative dans la Bible"*, 1959.

12 See Basil, *Epist.* 361 and 362. These letters form part of the corpus of the Basilian epistles. That there is no reason to doubt the authenticity of these letters is shown by G. L. Prestige, *St Basil the Great and Apollinaris of Laodicea*, 1956, and others (e.g. R. Weyenborg, 'De authenticitate et sensu quarundam epistolorum S. Basilio . . .', in *Antonianum* 33 (1958) 197-240, 371-414, and 34 (1959) 245-298). In any case the ideas expressed in these letters coincide fully with St Basil's theology found in the rest of his writings.

persons of the Holy Trinity. The question arose because, as St Basil states, some people accused those who accepted the *homoousios* of introducing "substance" as a principle in divine existence, either as ὑπερκείμενον or as ὑποκείμενον. This would correspond to the Platonic or an Aristotelian way of understanding the emergence of human beings. Apollinaris' reply seems to be fully acceptable to Basil and consists in the following significant thesis: there is no need to suppose either a "substance above" or a "substance underneath" the particular human beings, since human beings derive their being *not from a "common substance"* (κοινὴ ὑλή) *but from* the person of *Adam he* is the ἀρχή) and ὑπόθεσις(in other words the "cause") of us, and not human substance. Equally, he argues, in the case of God such a supposition of a substance either above or below is unnecessary, because it is *God the Father* (θεὸς ὁ πατή) and not divine οὐσία that is likewise the ἀρχή and ὑπόθεσις of divine being.

God's being, the Holy Trinity, is not caused by divine substance but by *the Father*, i.e. a particular being. The one God is the Father. Substance is something common to all three persons of the Trinity, but it is not ontologically primary until Augustine makes it so. The Cappadocians work out an ontology of divine being by employing the Biblical rather than the Greek view of being.[13]

2. Now, this can only make ontological sense if certain conditions apply. If Adam as a particular being and not as a human nature is the primary cause of human being, he must be in a *constant relationship* with all the rest of human beings, not via human nature — for this would make nature acquire again the decisive priority — but *directly*, i.e. as a particular being carrying in himself the *totality* of human nature, and not part of it.[14]

---

[13] Those who fail to appreciate the importance of the idea of 'cause' (αἴτιον), introduced by the Cappadocian Fathers to Trinitarian theology, apparently overlook these important implications of the matter. Unless the ontological ἀρχή in God is placed clearly and unequivocally *in a Person* — and who else but the Father could be such a person in the Trinity? — substance becomes the obvious candidate for such an ontological ἀρχή. This would leave the *homoousios* open to the accusations that prompted the above mentioned letters of St Basil and of course, would render an ontology of personhood problematic, if not altogether impossible.

[14] Cf. the concept of *perichoresis* with which the Cappadocians (Cf. Basil, *Ep.* 38, 8; Gregory Naz. or 31, 14) tried to express the unity of the Trinity: each person carries the full, undivided nature, and co-inheres in the other persons, thus showing substance to be commonly shared

The Fathers noted that this cannot be the case with Adam,[15] since death, owing to creaturehood, shows that the particular beings carry only part of human nature. Humanity, therefore, *per se* cannot be a candidate for personal ontology. But it is instructive to see in what way divinity is such a candidate. In God it is possible for the particular to be ontologically ultimate because *relationship is permanent and unbreakable*. Because the Father, the Son and the Spirit are always together,[16] the particular beings are bearers of the totality of nature and thus no contradiction between the 'one' and the 'many' can arise. What Adam *should* represent, God *does* represent.

This means that if we wish to build the particular into ontology we need to introduce *relationship* into substance itself, to make being relational.[17] In trying to identify a particular thing we have to make it part of a relationship and not isolate it as an *individual*, as the τόδε τί of Aristotle. This is a condition for an ontology of personhood. The result of such an ontology will be this:

The particular is raised to the level of ontological primacy, it emerges as *being itself* without depending for its identity on qualities borrowed from nature and thus applicable also to other beings, but solely on a relationship in which it constitutes an indispensable ontological ingredient, since it is inconceivable for the rest of beings to *be* outside a relationship with it. This results into a reality of communion in which each particular is affirmed as *unique* and irreplaceable by the others — a uniqueness which

among the persons not by way of each person holding *part* of it (note how the English word 'partaking' can be misleading as implying partition of nature), but by each *coinciding fully into one and the same nature*, carried *in its totality by each* person. It is a question of *unity of identity* of substance, (ταυτότης φύσεως: Didymus, *De Trin.* 1, 16), not of participation in a substance conceivable in itself as a kind of 'reservoir' of divine being. The tendency of Basil to speak at times of ὅμοια φύσις—which has led to his classification with the homoiousians — is to be seen in the light of his concern that the *homoousion* not be taken to imply partition of divine nature. This is evident also from the above mentioned *Epist.* 361.

[15] See again the correspondence between Basil and Apollinaris mentioned above. Cf. also Basil, *Epist.* 38, 4 and Gregory Naz. *Or.* 31, 11.

[16] Wherever one person of the Trinity is, the others are there, too. This is a basic patristic teaching related also to the idea of unity of God's *opera ad extra.* (See Athanasius, *Ad Serap.* I, 20; Basil, *De Spir. Sancto* 19, 49; Cyril of Alex. *In Joan.* 10).

[17] This kind of ontology was worked out, perhaps for the first time, by St Athanasius in his wrestling with the problems created by Arianism. More about this in our *Being as Communion*, 1985, p. 84 f.

is *ontological*, since the whole being in question depends on it, due to the unbreakable character of the relationship. If we define *love* in ontological terms, (i.e. as relationship creating absolute and unique identities) we must speak here of an ontology of love as replacing the ontology of οὐσία, i.e. we must attribute to love the role attributed to substance in classical ontology.

The overall consequence of this is that as long as ontology depends solely or ultimately on substance or nature it cannot accommodate the particular in an ultimate or primary way. This does not cause any problems with regard to the being of God (except in so far as theologians force into God's being the priority of substance in order to make it more intelligible to Man who as a creature is faced with the givenness of being, i.e. with the primacy of οὐσία or nature). God by being uncreated is not faced with given being: *He, as a particular being* (the Father) brings about His own being (the Trinity).[18] He is thus free in an ontological sense, and therefore the particular is primary in ontology in this case. But what about the human being?

3. The human being by asking the questions 'Who am I?' expects to raise the particular to the level of ontological primacy. This is built into this question of his being, as we have already seen. In so doing Man wishes to be God, for the conditions that we have set out for this ontology of personhood exist only in God. Is that the

---

[18] The question of whether God's being is constituted *freely* or not was already raised in the fourth century. By distinguishing will from substance and attaching the generation of the Son to God's substance and not to His will Athanasius provoked the accusation of the Arians that he was implying that the generation of the Son was not free but necessary. Athanasius (Cf. *Contra Ar.* 3, 66f.) replied by denying emphatically that the Father generated the Son 'unwillingly' (*atheletos*). Cyril of Alexandria offered a solution by stressing that, in God's being, will and substance are 'con-current' (*syndromos*), but it was mainly the Cappadocians, and in particular Gregory of Nazianzus who dealt successfully with this problem. In his *Orat. theol.* III, 5-7 Gregory distinguishes between 'will' (*thelesis*) and 'the willing one' (*ho thelon*). The significance of his position for our purpose here is twofold. On the one hand it implies that the question of freedom is a matter of *personhood*: God's being ultimately depends on a willing *person* — the Father; and on the other hand it indicates, as indeed Gregory explicitly states, that *even the Father's own being* is a result of the 'willing one' — the Father Himself. Thus by making a person — the Father — the ultimate point of ontological reference, the *aition*, the Cappadocian Fathers made it possible to introduce freedom into the notion of being, perhaps for the first time in the history of philosophy.

Imago Dei in Man? I believe it s. But the realisation of this drive of Man towards personal ontology cannot be provided by created being. Here *Christology* emerges as the only way of fulfilling the human drive to personhood. And this on the following conditions:

(a) That Christology is one *from above*, not from below. If 'above' stands for the uncreated — God — it is important to hold the view that Man acquires personal identity and ontological particularity only by basing his being in the Father-Son relationship in which nature is not primary to the particular being (owing to the fact that being is not 'given' — this is what 'uncreated' means). Chalcedon, therefore, made an important *ontological* statement in speaking of the hypostasis of the Son as the only personal identity of Christ.

(b) If this point concerning the priority of the particular in ontology is taken as a *sine qua non* condition, it emerges that in Christology the crucial thing for our subject is not the *communicatio idiomatum* but the hypostatic union. What enables Man in Christ to arrive at a personal identity in ontological terms is that in Christ the natures *are*, only because they are particularised in one person. In Christ the general exists only in and through the particular; the particular is thus raised to ontological primacy. The 'Who' of Christ is the Son. In Him the two natures give their qualities to the identity without making the identity depend in the primary ontological sense, on these qualities, i.e. in the sense in which our identities ultimately depend — and thus are unable to make the particular 'I' ontologically decisive. The natural qualities are not extrinsic to the identity — the question 'Who am I?' does not aim at excluding natural qualities from the identity of 'I' — but by being 'enhypostasized' these qualities become dependent on the hypostasis for their being; the hypostasis is not dependent on them. Thus the cause of being is the particular, not the general.

(c) For Man to acquire this ontology of personhood it is necessary to take an attitude of freedom *vis-à-vis* his own nature. If biological birth gives us a hypostasis dependent ontologically on nature, this indicates that a 'new birth' is needed in order to experience an ontology of personhood. This 'new birth', which is the essence of Baptism, is nothing but the acquisition of an identity not dependent on the qualities of nature but freely raising nature to a hypostatic existence identical with that which emerges from the Father-Son relationship. If Baptism gives 'sonship', the ontological significance of this is that Man's identity is now rooted not in the relations provided by nature, but in the uncreated Father-Son relationship.

(d) Finally, this identity can never be fully realised in history as long as nature still dictates its laws to Man, particularly in the form of death. When death ceases to be 'natural', humanity will experience the true ontology of the person. Meanwhile Man is called to preserve the image of God in him as much as possible, striving to free himself from the necessity of nature, experiencing 'sacramentally' the 'new being' as a member of the community of those 'born again' (in the above sense), and maintaining an eschatological vision and expectation of the transformation of the world. The ontology of personhood with all the conditions we have just outlined cannot be extrapolated from history or nature. If it exists and is not wishful thinking on man's part, it is the only 'analogy' or proof we have that God exists. If it does not exist, then our faith in God is untrue. Ontology in this situation is not applicable to personhood. We are left with a drive towards personal identity, which will be never fulfilled. Even so, it is worth keeping it at all costs. For without it Man ceases to be human.

III. Conclusions for an Ontology of Personhood

Who am I? This is a basically human question which no animal can raise. It is thus the question *par excellence* that makes us human and shows personhood to be an exclusive quality of the human being in the animal world. Even when it is not raised consciously (as it is raised in our Western culture), it conditions and colours every man's attitudes and activities whenever he, unlike the animals, is not satisfied with the given being and wishes to affirm freely identities of his own, thus creating his own world (e.g. in art, in unconditional love, in forgiveness, etc.)

In posing this question, however, man usually receives an answer point to *what* he is, not to *who* he is. This 'what' can take the form of a substantialist or idealist philosophy in which personal particularity is 'identified' — and thus lost — with ideas or ideals ultimately determining the human being. It can also take the naturalistic or biological form in which procreation of human species more or less is taken as identical with the emergence of persons. Connected with this is the problem of sex highlighted today by the Feminist movement. It is increasingly pointed out that women in our world feel a sort of loss of identity. To the question 'who am I?', posed by a woman, the implicit answer in our culture is essentially determined by sex: you are a woman. But this is an answer of 'what', not of 'who'.[19] How can we arrive at the pure 'who' answer to this question?

Our discussion here has pointed to the following observations:

(a) The 'who' question can never be totally divorced from the 'what' question in our created existence. This causes the difficulty in any attempt to create a true ontology of personhood. Nevertheless, it has to be always kept *distinct* from the 'what' question, if the human being is to remain truly human. Personhood is not about qualities or capacities of any kind: biological, social or moral. Personhood is about hypostasis, i.e. the claim to *uniqueness* in the absolute sense of the term, and this cannot be guaranteed by reference to sex or function or role, or even cultivated conscious- ness of the 'self' and its psychological experiences, since all of these can be *classified*, thus representing qualities shared by more than one being and not point to absolute uniqueness. Such qualities, important as they are for personal identity, become ontologically personal only through the hypostatisis to which they belong: only by being *my* qualities they are personal, but the ingredient "me" is a claim to absolute uniqueness which is not granted by these classifiable qualities constituting my "what", but by something else.

(b) Absolute uniqueness is indicated only through an affirmation arising freely from a relationship which constitutes by its unbrokenness the ontological ground of being for each person. In such a situation what matters ontologically is not 'what' one is but the very fact that he or she *is* and *not someone else*. The tendency of the Greek Fathers to avoid giving any positive content to the hypostases of the Trinity, by insisting that the Father is simply not the Son or the Spirit, and the Son means simply not the Father etc., points to the true ontology of hypostasis: that someone simply *is* and *is himself* and not someone else, and this is sufficient to identify him as a being in the true sense. This point acquires tremendous existential significance when placed in the context of ordinary human life. In relationships of genuine love, which are the proper context for the 'experience' of an ontology of personhood,

[19] Similar remarks apply to the identification of the 'who' of Man with, for example, 'a member of the working class', or 'a businessman' or any profession or social status. Even the identification with the 'ego' or the 'self', or the 'thinking agent' — categories used widely in modern depth psychology — can be reduced to the question of 'what' rather than that of 'who', as we have described it here.

one does not — and should not — identify the other with the help of their qualities (physical, social, moral, etc.), thus rejecting or accepting the other on that basis as a unique and irreplaceable partner in a relationship that matters ontologically (on which one's own personal identity depends). The more one loves ontologically and truly personally, the less one identifies someone as unique and irreplaceable for one's existence on the basis of such classifiable qualities. (In this case one rather loves *inspite* of the existence or absence of such qualities, just as God loves the sinner and recognizes him as a unique person.) Here it is perhaps appropriate to introduce into our terminology the category of *ethical apophatism*, so badly needed in our culture, with which to indicate that, exactly as the Greek Fathers spoke of the divine persons, we cannot give a *positive qualitative content* to a hypostasis or person, for this would result in the loss of his absolute uniqueness and turn a person into a classifiable entity. Just as the Father, the Son and the Spirit are not identifiable except simply through being who they are, in the same way a true ontology of personhood requires that the uniqueness of a person escape and transcend any qualitative *kataphasis*. This does not place personhood in the realm of a 'misty' mystery any more than the absence of a positive content in our reference to the persons of the Trinity does. Both in the case of God and of man the identity of a person is recognized and posited clearly and unequivocally, but this is so only in and through a *relationship*, and not through an objective ontology in which this identity would be *isolated*, pointed at and described in itself. Personal identity is totally lost if isolated, for its ontological condition is relationship.

This hypostatic fullness as otherness can emerge only through a relationship so constitutive ontologically that relating is not consequent upon being but is being itself. The *hypo-static* and the *ek-static* have to coincide.

2. Trinity, Ontology and Anthropology: Towards a Renewal of the Doctrine of the *Imago Dei*

Colin Gunton

I. Some Problems of Theological Anthropology

Two interrelated questions face the enquirer after a theological anthropology: the ontological and what can for want of a better term be called the comparative. The ontological question is the question about what kind of entity is the human, and has traditionally been answered in terms of a duality: of matter and spirit, body and soul, or the like; most radically perhaps in Descartes' famous dualism of intellectual mind and mechanical body. In Descartes, the ontological dimension is apparent: the human constitution reflects the dual structure of the universe as matter and (divine) idea. Mind, the godlike part of the person, is able by virtue of its equipment with innate ideas to comprehend by the use of pure reason the rational structure of the machine. In terms of anthropology, the outcome is that despite Descartes' attempts to show that his mind is more intimately related to his body than is a pilot to a ship, we are inescapably presented with the image of a mind pushing around a mechanical body. Ryle's characterisation of this as the 'ghost in the machine' is not so far from the mark.

The comparative enquiry concerns the way in which the human being is and is not like other entities supposed to people the universe: God on the one hand and, on the other, the non-human creation in all its various forms. The two questions are sometimes conflated, if not confused, by supposing that an argument for the distinctive ontology of the human might be derived from a comparison and contrast: by means of a quest for ways in which the human is different from other entities. Thus it might be held that God is infinite reason and the non-human creation is without reason, so that, on the one hand, the human is different from the divine by the virtue of its finitude, and, on the other, from the non-human by virtue of its possession of reason. We are here very near to the traditional form of the doctrine of the image of God, which

47

by being located in reason provides an answer to both of the questions with which we began. It is the possession of the image *as reason* which at once determines being and makes possible a comparative judgment both 'above' and below. Again, Descartes provides a fairly extreme example. The human mind, by virtue of its rationality, provides evidence both of a kind of image of God and at the same time a criterion of radical discontinuity from the rest of creation. The animals are merely machines, and it is said that some of the enlightened believed that their cries of pain were no more than the squeaks of unlubricated machinery.

But it is important to realise that the two questions do not have to be conflated. There are other ways of doing ontology than a process of speculative comparison and contrast: what Barth would call natural theology. Perhaps, as I shall argue, it is better to root contrast in ontology, and not the other way round. Moreover, it is in the long-lived tradition of rooting the image of God in reason that we see the deficiencies endemic in the tradition, deficiencies of which Descartes' anthropology provides but an example. A stress on reason elevates one characteristic of the human above others with equal claim to consideration as part of our being. In particular, it encourages the belief that we are more minds than we are bodies, with all the consequences that that has: for example, in creating a non-relational ontology, so that we are cut off from each other and from the world by a tendency to see ourselves as imprisoned in matter. (Spelled out, the two dimensions would lead us into the problems of individualism and ecology.)

The weakness in theological anthropology which is now so often observed can, accordingly, be seen to derive from errors of both method and content. Historically, the roots of the syndrome can be found in Irenaeus, whose anthropology in other dimensions takes so different a direction. In his famous distinction between image and likeness there began the process of making reason both a chief ontological characteristic and a criterion of difference between human and non-human.[1] By the time of Aquinas the tendency had hardened into a dogma. Perhaps most revealing is his citation of John of Damascus: 'being after God's image signifies his capacity for understanding, and for making free decisions and his mastery of himself'.[2] While that definition has the merit of not limiting the image to reason, it is to be noted that all of the characteristics are static possessions of the human as individual, rather than (say)

---

[1] See Emil Brunner, *Man in Revolt. A Christian Anthropology*, E.T. by Olive Wyon, London, 1939, 504.

[2] Aquinas, *Summa Theologiae*, 1a, 93.5.

characteristics implying relation. There remains, too, the problematic nature of the human relation to the rest of creation. The theological dimension of the problems can be discerned in Augustine. From the outset, there is in Augustine a tendency to develop anthropology in terms of neoplatonic categories. For him the human likeness to God must be in the mind or soul, so that other possibilities are excluded from the outset.[3] One implication is that our embodiedness cannot be the place where the image, and hence our true humanity, is found. That is a foreclosing of the ontological question which has a number of consequences. The first is a tendency to overstress the inner dimensions of the person. (I avoid here the words *intellectual* and *psychological* because their employment would prejudge questions about Augustine's meaning).[4] The second is equally important. Augustine's quest for the Trinity within the soul, the inner Trinity, risks reducing the Trinity to theological irrelevance, for it becomes difficult to ask in what way the doctrine of the Trinity may in other ways throw light on the human condition. The heart of the matter is perhaps in the doctrine of relations. Since relations are qualifications of the inner Trinity, and not relations between persons, it becomes difficult to see how the triune relatedness can be brought to bear on the central question of human relatedness. God's relatedness is construed in terms of self-relatedness,[5] with the result that it is as an individual that the human being is in the image of God, and therefore truly human. The outcome is another, theologically legitimated, version of the tendency to individualism which arises in every dimension of what has been said so far.

II. Cosmologies and Anthropologies

It is considerations such as those outlined in the previous section that give credence to Barth's critique of the theological respectability of natural theology. Certain approaches to theological anthropology have as a matter of fact been foreclosed because of a priori philosophical decisions. The difficulty with Barth's ap-

---

[3] See especially *De Trinitate* XI
[4] That the same kind of anthropology is with us still is evident from the number of modern attempts to ground humanity in such features of our experience as consciousness, inwardness and subjectivity.
[5] In that respect, Kierkegaard's anthropology bears many of the marks of Augustine. See *Sickness unto Death*, E.T. by Walter Lowrie, Princeton U.P., 1954, 147: 'by relating itself to its own self and by willing to be itself the self is grounded transparently in the power which posited it'.

proach, however, is that it leaves out certain stages of argument which seem to be advisable in the modern context if an appearance of authoritarianism is to be avoided. The time has therefore come to ask whether an approach that is different from either the traditional or the straightforwardly 'Barthian' can be attempted. The question can be approached indirectly, with the observation that different theories about the kind of entity that the world is bring in their train different conceptions of what it is to be human. That is to say, we can observe the way in which as a matter of fact cosmologies have been correlative with anthropologies. At its most simple level, the matter can be illustrated with the help of the distinction often made between Old Testament cosmologies and others of the Ancient Near East. While the latter tended to conceive the world as born from the womb of deity or developed from deity's defeated body — thus suggesting the at least potential deity of aspects of the world — the former, by distinguishing more definitely between God and what he had made, suggested a different view of the place of the human creature: more unified, and with fewer pretensions to deity. In later thought, a similar distinction emerges between broadly Greek and Hebrew views of the person.

While not wishing to give simplistic views of their distinction, I want to begin with an account of a general difference. In *The Greeks and the Irrational*, E. R. Dodds traces the origins of Greek cosmological anthropology to the myth of the Titans. These were the giants who slew, cooked and ate the body of the infant Dionysus. In revenge, Zeus slew the Titans, from whose smoking ruins there derived the human race. Underlying that legend are the roots of an essentially dualistic ontology which can be said to be almost universal in Greek thought and, through Augustine, though with qualifications, highly influential for Christian anthropology. The duality suggested is to be found on the one hand in the evil matter from which the human race arises; and on the other from the fragment of deity deriving from the ingested divinity ('the horrid tendencies of the Titans, tempered by a tiny portion of divine soul-stuff').[6] Therein, undoubtedly is to be found the basis of the doctrine that the defining characteristic of humanity or the place of the image of God is reason.

A more developed philosophical treatment of the dualism is to be found in Plato. In the *Republic's* discussion of the tripartite soul, Plato is not far from suggesting that embodiment is in itself

[6]   E. R. Dodds, *The Greeks and the Irrational*, University of California Press, 1951, 155.

a form of fallenness.[7] Physical desires and appetites are for the most part a bad thing, to be sternly controlled by reason. But for our purposes, the interesting discussion comes in the *Phaedo*. There we find the repeated assertion that the body is a prison, and death the liberation from it. The true philosopher abstains from pleasures and pains, each of which fastens the soul to the body with a kind of rivet, contaminating the soul in the process. Similarly, the soul is naturally immortal, because it resembles the divine, while the body resembles mortal things.[8] Overall, the message is clear: with a dualistic cosmology, a dualistic anthropology is likely to be correlative.

But it is a mistake simply to contrast a Greek dualism with a more Hebrew or unitary approach. Monism is a problem, too. Something more sophisticated and complex than a simple opposition is required, and that is why Carver Yu, whose recent diagnosis of Western individualism is so good, cannot solve the problem by simply opposing to it a biblical and relational ontology, as he tends to do in the final chapter of the book.[9] For a more subtle diagnosis of the possibilities we turn to Coleridge. In *On the Prometheus of Aeschylus* he offers an immensely valuable three-fold typology of world-views. There are, he says, three available cosmologies, not just two. (That is to say, he will not simply oppose 'Greek' and 'Hebrew', monist and dualist.) The first he calls the 'Phoenician'. According to this, 'the cosmogony was their theogony and *vice versa*'. That is to say, the origin of the cosmos and the origin of the divine are one and the same process. What emerges is a conception of the world as a kind of undifferentiated unity. We have an equation containing only two terms: 'a self-organising chaos' and '. . . nature as the result'.[10]

Moving on from Coleridge, or rather moving on to concerns he expressed in other writings than this, we might see in pantheism the typical modern version of this form of cosmology. According to Spinoza, for example, the coming to be of God of the world are one and the same thing, except of course that in Spinoza's timeless system to speak of a cosmogony is perhaps not easy: nonetheless, his cosmogony is his theogony. The Coleridgean objection to such cosmologies can be seen in Spinoza's view that we can no more do

[7] Plato, *Republic*, 436ff.
[8] Plato, *Phaedo* 83b, 80a.
[9] Carver T. Yu, *Being and Relation. A Theological Critique of Western Dualism and Individualism*, Edinburgh, 1987.
[10] Samuel Taylor Coleridge, 'On the Prometheus of Aeschylus', Complete Works, ed. W. G. T. Shedd, London, 1853, Vol. IV, 353, 354f.

other than we in fact do than the angles of a triangle can choose to be less or more than 180°. The outcome is the absolute necessitarian determinism that Coleridge saw to be enemy of human personality and freedom. Similarly, if we consider the description of the chaos as 'self-organising' we may think of the implications for anthropology of an effective divinisation of the process of evolution. The authoritarian tendency of some of Teilhard de Chardin's work has sometimes been suggested, and in this context we can see why. In a 'Phoenician' cosmology, the person is not separable from the world, and so lacks the space to be free.

Coleridge's second cosmology, which he names the Greek, differs in that it has three rather than two terms. It is midway between the Phoenician and the Hebrew. It does assume a divinity 'antecedent to the matter of the world. But on the other hand it coincides with the Phoenician in considering this antecedent ground . . . not so properly the cause of (corporeal matter), as the occasion and the still continuing substance. . . . The corporeal was supposed co-essential with the antecedent of its corporeity'.[11] That is where Prometheus comes into Coleridge's conception of things. The 'fire' Prometheus steals from heaven is mind, the 'form', the incipient or potential divinity, which shapes human nature. (A modernised equivalent, we might say, of the fragment of divinity remaining in the immolated Titans). There are important and positive anthropological implications, of which Coleridge is aware: mind, being stolen from heaven, is 'no mere evolution of the animal basis', and reveals the distinction between the human and the other creation. But that, as we have seen, is also the beginning of danger. In some respects, as Coleridge points out 'the Greek philosopheme does not differ essentially from the cosmotheism, or identification of God with the universe. . . .'[12]

In general, the Greek cosmology has a number of problems. John Zizioulas has pointed one: 'In platonic thought the person is a concept which is ontologically impossible, because the soul, which ensures man's continuity, is not united permanently with the concrete "individual" man . . .' (p. 28). Platonic thought cannot handle concrete relatedness: the godlike part of us excludes relations with others through the medium of our embodiedness, because our bodies are what *separate* what is really ourselves — the 'inner' — from others of us. (The concept of love in the *Symposium* is the logical outcome.) Similarly, the continuity with the divine that is implied brings problems for the divine-human

[11] Coleridge, op. cit., 354.
[12] Coleridge, op. cit., 360.

relationship. As relations with other finite creatures are too distant through lack of relationship, here there is a danger that the relation will be too close. To be godlike in the wrong sense is a great burden, and the nature of the human image of the divine has to be handled very carefully if the burden is to be avoided. We require space as well as relation: to be both related to and other than those and that on which we depend.[13]

III. Space to be human: the Trinity

Coleridge believes the Hebrew view of things to be related to the Greek, which, as we have seen, he regards as a mid-point between the Phoenician and Hebrew, but superior. It is, first of all, mathematically superior, in that it has four terms in contrast to the preceding two and three. (Coleridge was perhaps too enamoured of mathematics, but at least the point can be taken that the greater possibilities of the four term conceptuality allows for greater ontological richness and openness). The four are as follows: the self-sufficient immutable creator; the antecedent night; the chaos; the material world resulting from the divine fiat. It is not very clear what is meant by all this, but some light can be shed by moving from the *Prometheus* to a consideration of Coleridge's theory of the Trinity in general. That is to say, we reach the place where we must go beyond the general matter of celebrating the Hebrew over against other cosmologies, and ask more particularly about the doctrine of God.

The idea of the Trinity was for Coleridge the transcendental of transcendentals, that which served as the supreme mark, determinant perhaps, of being. The Trinity is 'that *Idea Idearum*, the one substrative truth which is the form, manner and involvement of all truths. . . .'[14] Nor by *idea* did he simply mean, as so many of his British predecessors had done, simply a mental construct or concept. As he shows in *On the Constitution of the Church and State*, an idea is antecedent to a conception, and has an (almost?) ontological status. It is, indeed, a kind of conception, but one 'which is not abstracted from any particular state, form, or mode, in which the thing may happen to exist at this or at that time; but

---

13 I owe the concept of space used in this context to Daniel Hardy, 'Coleridge on the Trinity', *Anglican Theological Review*, LXIX, 1988, 145-155.

14 Coleridge, 'Notes on Waterland's Vindication of Christ's Divinity', *Complete Works*, op. cit., Vol. V, 407.

which is given by the knowledge of *its ultimate aim*.' Interestingly for our purpose, Coleridge, in discussing one instance of idea, that 'of an ever-originating social contract', argues that it is dependent on 'the yet higher idea of *person*, in contra-distinction from *thing* . . . .'.[15] *Person* is somewhere near the top of the hierarchy of ideas, yet, remarkably, all such ideas are in some way or other subordinate to the transcendental of transcendentals, the Trinity.

In his paper 'Coleridge on the Trinity', Daniel Hardy has spelled out some of the developments in Coleridge's doctrine of the Trinity after the *Prometheus* essay. Attempting to free himself from the 'restrictive notion of space-like being' to be found in that essay, Coleridge turned to the will as the clue to the Trinity. What he was seeking was a ground for reality without any of the anti-personal implications that follow from the rejected alternatives. Hardy quotes from the *Opus Maximum*: 'If then personeity, by which term I mean the source of personality, be necessarily contained in the idea of the perfect will, how is it possible that personality should not be an essential attribute of this will, contemplated as self-realized.'[16] The Augustinian and individualistic form of that formulation is manifest, but so also is its instinctive feeling for the right questions. Coleridge knew that if there was to be personality, there had to be both relatedness and space at once between God and the world and within the world between finite persons. He was not here concerned with narrowly pragmatic matters, but with the real, which 'had to be seen in its connection to its foundation'.[17] His quest for the idea of the Trinity was a quest for that which would enable him both to think the real and to show the bearing of that reality on life in the world. At the very least, there is a concern for conceptualising a kind of space between God and the world, a space in which personal freedom operates.

I have suggested by frequent use of the concept that underlying Coleridge's schematism is a concern for space in which the human can be human. According to the Phoenician scheme, there is no space between God and the world, and so no human freedom. According to the kind of Hellenism we have viewed, the space is located in the wrong place: between mind and matter, so that there is too little space between the human mind and God too much between one person and another: space is here at the expense of relation. In the third, Hebrew, scheme, there is space,

---

[15] Coleridge, *On the Constitution of the Church and State, The Collected Works of Samuel Taylor Coleridge*, ed. John Colmer, London, 1976, 20, 12, 15.

[16] Hardy, op. cit., 155.

[17] Hardy, op. cit., 148.

because of the freedom of the immutable God to create *ex nihilo*. But we need more than space. Indeed, from one point of view, space is the problem: individualism is the view of the human person which holds that there is so much space between people that they can in no sense participate in each other's being. There is clearly space and space, and our requirement now to find a conception which is correlative with that of relation.

IV. In the Image of God

On a more articulated account of the Trinity than Coleridge in practice allowed, we shall have to give prominence to the concept of the person rather than personeity. Only thus shall we avoid the monism that Coleridge so rightly feared, but risked by his emphasis on the will. *Person* is here difficult to define: if it is indeed one of those *ideas* which are logically primitive because they reflect what is ontologically primitive, that is what we should expect. Such concepts cannot be defined in other terms, because they are the *ideas*, and I continue to use the italics to indicate Coleridge's technical sense, in terms of which other concepts can and must be understood. But that is not to say that they can in no way be *thought*. They can, for example, be thought when they are found to be concretely instantiated in particular forms of life. Classically, they came to be thought *theologically* under the impact of the Christian gospel. As a result the Greek theologians came to understand God as a communion of persons, each distinct but inseparable from the others, whose being consists in their relations with one another. As Barth said, but in a rather different way, *person* means primarily what it means when it is used of God.[18] But before we can take up this suggestion, asking what the

[18] Karl Barth, *Church Dogmatics*, II/1, E.T. by G. W. Bromiley, Edinburgh, T. & T. Clark, 1975, 272. Compare Wolfhart Pannenberg, 'The Question of God,' *Basic Questions in Theology*, Volume Two, E.T. by G. H. Kehm, London: SCM Press, 1971, 230: 'If the concept of the personal is originally based upon a religiously determined experience of reality ...'. The famous and futile Western quest for analogies of the Trinity in the created world (such as those listed by Barth in *Church Dogmatics* I/1, 343f) can in this light be understood as an attempt to follow up some of the possibilities of the logical primitiveness of trinitarian thinking. Their weakness is their employment as attempts to illustrate the divine Trinity: the world is used to throw light on God, rather than the other way round, so that attention falls on irrelevances like the number three rather than on the personal nature of the triune God.

theological concept of person contributes to the understanding of the finite person, we must first ask a preliminary question: how, in the light of Coleridge's third possibility, the trinitarian, are we enabled to see the world and human life within it? Is there here too a kind of cosmology within which anthropological possibilities may be articulated?

What flows from the conception of God as three persons in communion, related but distinct? First, there is something of the space we have been seeking. We have a conception of *personal space*: the space in which three persons are for and from each other in their otherness. They thus confer particularity upon and receive it from one another. That giving of particularity is very important: it is a matter of space to be. Father, Son and Spirit through the shape — the *taxis* — of their inseparable relatedness confer particularity and freedom on each other. That is their personal being.

What is the outcome when we turn in the light of such a doctrine of God to the theology of creation? Creation becomes understood as the giving of being to the other, and that includes the giving of space to be: to be other and particular. Much is made in recent cosmology of the singularity — particularity — of our universe. It is what it is and not another thing because of the unique conditions that gave it the space-time shape that it has. But we should also note that recent science has much to say about the interrelatedness of all that is. We need not claim that such teaching necessarily derives from the doctrine of creation or even that it is in some way related to it, although claims, frequently made, that modern science is in some way causally related to the Christian doctrine of creation may have some justification. (Note that some of Einstein's difficulties with quantum theory derived from his own rather Spinozistic concept of God.) The point is that the world's otherness from God is part of its space to be itself, to be finite and not divine. But it as such also echoes the trinitarian being of God in being what it is by virtue of its internal taxis: it is, like God, a dynamic of beings in relation.

Yet to claim creation's particularity and contingency, even its own kind of freedom, is not the same as to say that it is made in the image of God, unless with the philosophers of Process we are to conclude that those beings in relation are all in some sense personal. Rather, creation's non-personality means that it is unable to realise its destiny, the praise of its creator, apart from persons. It is not personal, but requires persons in order to be itself. That is why it awaits with eager longing the revealing of the children of God (Romans 8.19). It is in some such context as this that we have to seek for the outlines of a theological anthropology.

One of the sources of recent controversy in cosmology has been the anthropic principle, which at the very least suggests a necessary relatedness of the cosmos to human intelligence. It would be a mistake to try to take this speculative principle to be evidence that the world is created for the production of human life, though that may as a matter of fact be the case. But at the very least, recent discussions encourage us to conceive a positive relation between human rationality and the structure of the universe. On its own, such an approach leads only to a repetition of the problematic which I outlined at the outset: of an attempt to read off from some naturally observed feature of the world a difference — and, indeed, a difference consisting in reason — between human and non-human which then becomes definitive of the difference between not only the two but also the human and the divine. If, then, we are to pursue theologically the question of the way in which the cosmos provides a context for anthropology, further intermediate steps are needed in the argument.

To put the question another way: what in all this are we to make of the doctrine of the image of God? Given the rejection of the view that the image is to be found in reason, or any merely internal characterisation of the individual, there seem to be two recent contenders for the title, both dependent upon readings of the first two chapters of Genesis. The first locates it in the human stewardship of the creation.[19] There is much to be said for this approach, especially in view of the close relationship in Genesis between the creation of humankind and the command to shepherd the earth. Such a theology is, however, too literalistic and too restricted, especially in the light of the New Testament reorienting of the doctrine to Christ. Is the image of God as realised in Christ to be expressed in terms of his stewardship of the creation — indeed, part of the matter — or must other things also be said? We must here remember that the concept of image has in this respect very little biblical employment, and if it is to be used theologically must draw upon a wider range of biblical background than such explicit talk of image as there is in scripture.

The second candidate for the interpretation of image interprets it with Genesis' 'male and female created he them'. Barth, famously, creatively and controvenially pursued this approach, which was developed in somewhat less literalistic style by Derrick Sherwin Bailey.[20] The weaknesses of this approach, Barth's par-

---

[19] Hans Walter Wolff, *Anthropology of the Old Testament*, E.T. by Margaret Kohl, London, 1974, ch. xviii; Douglas John Hall, *Imaging God. Dominion as Stewardship*, Grand Rapids, 1986.

[20] Barth, *Church Dogmatics* III/1 and Derrick Sherwin Bailey, *The Man Woman Relation in Christian Thought*, London, 1959, 268ff.

ticularly, have often been pointed. Two should be rehearsed. The first is its tendency to be binitarian: the anthropology reflects a Father-Son duality reflected in that of male and female, rather than expressing a theology of communion. That is not to say that there is nothing of anthropology of communion in Barth. The anthropology of mutuality in *Church Dogmatics* III/2 is immensely illuminating, as are many of the things he says about man-woman relations, despite their unpalatability to a certain kind of feminism. The second weakness is a tendency to anthropocentrism in Barth. Andrew Linzey's analysis of Barth's treatment of the creation sagas has shown that Barth underplays the way in which Genesis brings the non-human creation into the covenant.[21] We need more than an extended exegesis of Gen. 1.26f, and in particular a broader treatment of the topic, if we are really to make more satisfactory use of the concept of the *imago dei*.

Where, then, is the image of God to be found? Interesting about the two alternatives we have reviewed is that while one of them relates humankind to the cosmos, the other is chiefly concerned with relations within the human species. It is an unsatisfactory theological anthropology which requires a choice between the two, which are both right insofar as they discern in relatedness a clue to the solution of the problem. The weakness of both approaches can be obviated by finding a concept which bases them — and any other dimensions — in a theological ontology. Insofar as we are concerned with human *being* and not particular qualities or tasks there is a missing conceptual link to be found: it is, of course, that of the person. To be made in the image of God is to be endowed with a particular kind of personal reality. To be a person is to be made in the image of God: that is the heart of the matter. If God is a communion of persons inseparably related, then surely Barth is thus far correct in saying that it is in our relatedness to others that our being human consists.

That relatedness takes shape in a double orientation. In the first place, we are persons insofar as we are in right relationship to God. Under the conditions of sin, that means, of course, insofar as the image is reshaped, realised, in Christ. But since we are here enquiring about human createdness, we shall leave that in the background, as a very real background, nevertheless. The relation to God takes shape through the Son and the Spirit. To be in the image of God is to be created through the Son, who is the archetypal bearer of the image. To be in the image of God therefore

21 Andrew Linzey, *The Neglected Creature. The Doctrine of the Non-human Creation and its Relation with the Human in the Thought of Karl Barth*, PhD, University of London, 1986.

means to be conformed on the person of Christ. The agent of this conformity is God the Holy Spirit, the creator of community. The image of God is then that being human which takes shape by virtue of the creating and redeeming agency of the triune God.

The second orientation is the 'horizontal' one, and is the outcome of the work of the first. What is the shape that the image of God takes in time? The human person is one who is created to find his or her being in relation, first with other like persons but second, as a function of the first, with the rest of the creation. This means, first, that we are in the image of God when, like God but in dependence on his giving, we find our reality in what we give to and receive and from others in human community. One way into the content of the image, its concrete realisation, is through the concept of love. It seems likely that we shall be content here neither with the unitive concept of love which has tended to reign in the West, nor with the strong reaction signalled in Nygren's one-sided assertion of *agape* against *eros*. While it seems to me that *agape* does indeed reflect the biblical expression of the divine self-giving in Christ, to stress that alone can lead to an almost individualistic unrelatedness. Barth here is better when he sees our humanity as realised in the mutual giving and receiving of assistance with gladness.[22]

But if we are to speak of realising our being in relations, something more than that has to be said. Of crucial importance is the matter of the way in which the structure — the taxis — of human community constitutes the particularity, uniqueness and distinctness of persons: their free otherness in relation. To be a person is to be constituted in particularity and freedom — to be given space to be — by others in community. *Otherness* and *relation* continue to be the two central and polar concepts here. Only where both are given due stress is personhood fully enabled. Their co-presence will rule out both the kind of egalitarianism which is the denial of particularity, and leads to collectivism, and forms of individualism which in effect deny humanity to those unable to 'stand on their own feet'.

It is important also to realise that this being in the image of God will embrace both what we have been used to call spiritual and our bodiliness. The merit of the approach to anthropology by means of the concept of person is that it relativises so many inherited dualisms. Relations are of the whole person, not of minds or bodies alone, so that from all those created in the image of God there is something to be received, and to them something to be given.

[22] Karl Barth, *Church Dogmatics* III/2, 265.

When the image is located in reason, or for that matter in any internal qualification like consciousness, problems like those of 'other minds' are unavoidable. The person as a being in relation is one whose materiality is in no way *ontologically* problematic, whatever problems derive from the way in which we relate in actual fact to others.

The contention that our realising of the image of God embraces our embodiedness as much as our intellect and 'spirituality' leads into the further point that we are not human apart from our relation with the non-personal world. Much current misuse of the creation, with its attendant ecological disasters, derives from a lack of realisation of human community with the world. It is not the same kind of community, that of equals, as that with which we were concerned when speaking of the community of persons. But it is a fact that we receive much of what we are from the world in which we are set and from whose dust we come. It is the context within which we become persons, and it, too, is in a kind of community with us, being promised a share in the final reconciliation of all things. Although it is not itself personal, the non-human creation is bound up with that of the human, and depends upon us for its destiny. It is not something we stand over against in the sense that it is at our arbitrary disposal, as 'technocracy' assumes. It is rather, to use Polanyi's metaphor, the reality which we indwell bodily, intellectually and spiritually. Here, being in the image of God has something to do with the human responsibility to offer the creation, perfected, back to its creator as a perfect sacrifice of praise. It is here that are to be found the elements of truth in the claims that the image of God is to be found in the human stewardship of the creation.

In all of this, John Zizioulas' point that *person* is an eschatological concept must constantly be borne in mind. To say that is to say that personhood is being that is to be realised, and whose final realisation will come only when God is all in all. And yet, as Graham McFarlane's paper shows, that need not be taken to undermine the fact that it is also, and without inconsistency, a protological concept. It is a way of conceptualising the origins of human being in the creating goodness of God, though without prejudice to the dynamic orientation of this being to a purposed end. Irenaeus' theory that Adam and Eve were created childlike is not in every way satisfactory, but it does suggest that human life in the image of God is human life directed to an end. The image is not a static possession, but comes to be realised in the various relationships in which human life is set. The New Testament's reorientation of the concept to Jesus makes the point well. It is because Jesus is 'the image of the invisible God' that God is 'through him to reconcile all things, whether on earth or in heaven ...' (Col. 1.15, 20). The one through whom all was created is also the means of the re-establishment of the image in humanity. The image, therefore, created through the Word and in the Spirit, has in like manner to be realised through them, between the resurrection of Jesus and his return in glory.

V. Conclusion

The paper began with the linking of two questions: the ontological and the comparative. What kind of being is the human? In what ways is the human species like and unlike God? We have come to answers rather unlike those of much of the tradition. *Ontologically*, it has been argued that where the latter tended to stress the non-bodily, a trinitarian theology will stress the relations which involve all dimensions of our reality. Where the tradition tended to see our imagedness to consist in the possession of certain faculties, here the stress is on the ontology of personhood. To be in the image of God is at once to be created as a particular kind of being — a person — and to be called to realise a certain destiny. The shape of that destiny is to be found in God-given forms of human community and of human responsibility to the universe.

The *comparative* question also finds a different kind of answer. Human difference from the rest of the creation does not lie in some absolute ontological distinction, but in an asymmetry of relation, and therefore a relative difference. As created beings, human persons are bound up closely with the fate of the rest of the material universe, as stewards rather than absolute lords. And the difference between God and those made in his image? The interesting point now is that the question of our difference from and likeness to God becomes less pressing. It is not found in some structural difference, but in the most basic one of all: God is the creator, we are of his creation. The triune God has created humankind as finite persons-in-relation who are called to acknowledge his creation by becoming the persons they are and by enabling the rest of the creation to make its due response of praise.

II

Historical and Systematic Studies

1. Person as Confession: Augustine of Hippo

Brian L. Horne

In 1894 the Bampton Lectures were delivered by the highly-regarded and widely-read Christian philosopher J. R. Illingworth.[1] His subject was *Personality, Human and Divine*, and the first lecture was entitled 'Development of the Conception of Human Personality'. After a brief glance at the concept of personality in the philosophical thought of classical Greece he announces that 'the real foundations of our subsequent thought upon the point were undoubtedly laid in the first Christian centuries, and chiefly by Christian hands'.[2] At first sight it is a claim that seems to bear a remarkable similarity to that made much more recently by John Zizioulas in his essay 'Personhood and Being' that the person 'both as a concept and as living reality is purely the product of patristic thought'.[3] But Illingworth continued in a vein very different from that of Zizioulas for he does not mention the Cappadocian Fathers (central to Zizioulas's thesis) or dwell very long in the patristic period at all and so reaches a very different conclusion about what personality, both human and divine, means. Illingworth's attention is fixed firmly upon the Church in the West and the Western tradition of Christian philosophy.

> It is, of course, impossible to trace minutely the development of an idea whose elements gradually coalesced, as floating things are drawn together in the vortex of a stream. Many minds and many influences contributed to the result, while the monasteries provided homes for introspective meditation. But for con-

---

[1] One of the moving spirits behind the publication of *Lux Mundi* (1889), Illingworth contributed two essays to this 'landmark in the history of English theological thought'. (S. C. Carpenter, *Church and People 1789-1889*). Later books included *Divine Immanence* (1898), *Reason and Revelation* (1902) and *The Doctrine of the Trinity*. In the spirit of *Lux Mundi* he saw himself — and was seen by others — as representing an enlightened and 'modern' orthodox position in matters of Christian doctrine — and philosophy.

[2] *Personality. Human and Divine*, p. 13.

[3] *Being as Communion. Studies in Personhood and the Church*, p. 11.

venience of summary and memory three names may perhaps be singled out, as at least typical, if not actually creative, of the chief epochs, through which the conception of personality has passed — Augustine, Luther, Kant.[4]

He says of Kant, a few pages later, that apart from his origins in Augustine and Luther he had predecessors in Descartes and Leibniz; and I have no doubt that he is correct in that assertion. That is not our concern. What does concern us is that he confidently traces a continuous line of thought back from Descartes (and so from Kant and the modern era) to its origin in Augustine. So he writes:

> Descartes, whether consciously or unconsciously, following out the thought of Augustine, had enunciated his famous maxim, 'Cogito ergo sum,' I think, therefore I am - Thought, that is to say, is the evidence of its own reality, and of the real existence of its thinker, the individual man.[5]

Now Illingworth was no disciple of Kant, but he has in mind, as he writes his lectures, an audience whose philosophical development and understanding — even in England — was deeply imbued with Kantianism. He openly acknowledges that 'it was Kant who inaugurated the modern epoch in the treatment of personality' and he seems to accept without question the notion of 'the personal' being rooted in individual self-consciousness, that is the power of separating oneself as a subject from oneself as an object. '. . . all knowledge is due to the activity of the subject, or ego, or self, in bringing the multiplicity of external facts or internal feelings into relation with its own central unity. . . .'[6] This definition of human personality has profound consequences for his perception of Divine personality and his understanding of the relations between the members of the Holy Trinity.

When Illingworth comes to deal with the image of God in man, however, it is not so much in Reason that he locates this image, that is not in Reason as a kind of faculty in the human individual which sets him apart from the rest of creation as a kind of god-like being, but in the essentially tripartite nature of human consciousness. And his reference here is, not to the Augustine of *De Trinitate* but the Augustine of the *Confessions*. 'I exist, I am conscious, I will. I exist as conscious and willing, I am conscious of existing and

---

[4] Ibid., pp. 13-14.
[5] Ibid., p. 20.
[6] Ibid., p. 21.

willing, I will to exist and be conscious; and these three functions, though distinct are inseparable and form one life, one mind, one essence' (*Confessions*, Book XIII, ch. II). And turning to the notion of Divine Personality he feels able to say that '. . . we start from the fact that our belief in a Personal God is founded on an instinctive tendency, morally and philosophically developed'.[7] Not, we may note, in the *first* instance, founded upon a belief in a Divinity which reveals itself in such a way that it can be encountered personally or recognized and worshipped as tri-personal. That was the Cappadocian approach and Illingworth, like most of the classical thinkers of the Western tradition is too firmly rooted in the thought of Augustine for that. His approach to the definition of Divine Personality must be by the way of the analogy of the self-reflectiveness of the discrete human personality; itself the product of a theory of personhood which took shape in one of the most remarkable books of Western European literature: Augustine's *Confessions*.

It is a book as puzzling as it is remarkable, and is remarkable (partly) because it presents us with such puzzles. Why should have Augustine assumed, at the age of forty-three, that anyone would be interested in his 'spiritual' development? Are we convinced that he wrote in order 'to persuade his admirers that any good qualities he had were his by the grace of God. . . .'[8] Did he really have an audience in mind? We are in a position to know exactly why Jean-Jacques Rousseau wrote his *Confessions* and John Henry Newman his *Apologia*, but the creative origin of Augustine's autobiographical work remains obscure. It is true that he begins the tenth book with an address to God in which an intention is declared. It is, what might be called, a moral intention; it is for the encouragement of others: he hopes and prays that those who read his book will have their hearts turned to God. But can we be satisfied with this? The writing burns with such idiosyncratic intensity that the reader is ineluctably drawn into the soul of the writer. We are invited to *know* Augustine and not merely be uplifted and illuminated by his example. In this the work is unique in its own age and we can be sure that more is being conveyed by the writer and demanded of the reader than the author openly admits or even perhaps recognizes.

One of the most illuminating analyses of the *Confessions* is to be found in a long essay written by Rebecca West in 1933. She was

---

[7] Ibid., p. 76.
[8] See e.g. the Introduction by R. S. Pine-Coffin to his translation of Augustine's *Confessions*.

clearly fascinated by the figure of Augustine and began with the assertion that Augustine 'is one of the greatest of all writers, and he works in the same introspective field as the moderns. In his short, violent sentences, which constantly break out in the rudest tricks of the rhetoricians, rhymes, puns, and assonances, he tries to do exactly what Proust tries to do in his long reflective sentences. . . . He tries to take a cast of his mental state at a given moment. . . . Nevertheless, we must not take the *Confessions* as altogether faithful to reality. It is too subjectively true to be objectively "accurate".[9] That last statement, together with the reference to *A la Recherche du Temps perdu,* give the clue to what is 'going on' in the *Confessions.* I believe that the book was written, though he denies it, for himself, that he had no specific audience in mind, and that he was creating something that was both unique and destined to become a model. (I might add that we know, accurately, what kind of audiences Rousseau, Newman and even Proust had in mind, but that they could have an audience at all arises out of the possibility created, almost accidentally, by the *Confessions* of Augustine.)

What, then, is 'going on' in the *Confessions?* We see not merely, as Rebecca West observed, the attempt of a man 'to take a cast of his mental state at a given moment', but much more: the deliberate creation of a 'persona', the 'I' or subject of the narrative. It is no accident that so many writers on 'narrative theology' go to Augustine's *Confessions* as a primary text, the classic example (outside the Biblical text) of the genre of 'narrative theology'. It does exactly what narrative theologians want a text to do: it presents a theology by telling a story, or, perhaps, to put it the other way around, it tells a story in such a way that the theological implications are unmistakable. We take this further: in the *Confessions* we have the attempt at discovering meaning in a life and imposing an order on chaos by means of relating and forming into a narrative (a human history) selected pieces of previous experience. It is, in a real sense, the re-creation of the person by the recollection of the past; and the process by which this is done is highly selective.

The comparison with Proust now becomes instructive. In *A la Recherche du Temps Perdu* the narrator, Marcel, in middle-age confronts the meaninglessness of his own existence. The sense of personal identity has dissolved and is connected with the awareness

---

[9]   *Rebecca West: A Celebration,* pp. 165-166. The essay, *St. Augustine,* was originally published in 1933.

of loss, the loss of the past, more specifically, the loss of his own past. There seems to be no connection between the Marcel of the present in rain-soaked Paris and the boy in the house at Combray, or between any of the Marcels who have appeared at various stages of the author's life. Significantly, it can only be by a private, interior journey in the memory that meaning can be found. Time that is lost must be recovered; the past of the narrator must be related significantly to the present. Only when that has been accomplished can meaning release itself into the narrator's perception of the world and personal identity be achieved. However, this cannot be done by the writing of a chronicle, the mere recollection and cataloguing of events with as much historical accuracy as possible; it is the shaping of the remembered events in a narrative form that bestows meaning and a renewed grasp of one's personhood.[10] One is, so to speak, the story one tells oneself. One constructs one's personality in the telling of the story, and does not know oneself until one's story is told. The unacknowledged, perhaps unknown model for this modern masterpiece is Augustine's *Confessions*. Proust completed and brought to an unimagined apotheosis something which had begun fifteen centuries earlier: a comprehensive description and demonstration of what it means to be a person.

It is obvious that memory is central to the whole enterprise; and the centre of gravity of the *Confessions* is the tenth book. This contains a long meditation on the operation of memory. Augustine tells us that he is both fascinated and bewildered by it, especially in the connection there seems to be between the power of the faculty and the realization of personal identity. In his memory lie not only all the images of everything in the external world that have ever impinged upon his senses, but his own past self experiencing the impact of the external world. He ponders on the difference between the immediate experience of the sensations and the recollected experience and wonders if there is a similar distinction between the immediate awareness of the self in the present and recollection of what the self has been. This is particularly puzzling in the case of remembered emotion:

[10] '. . . the past and the present aren't in strict sequence. . . . They are, obviously in the calendar sense, but they're not in that sequence in your head, and neither are they in terms of the way you discover things about yourself. An event of 20 years ago can follow yesterday instead of preceding it, and out of this morass of evidence, the clues, searchings and strivings, which is the metaphor for the way we live, we can start to put up the structure called self. Then we can walk out of that structure, saying, at least I and you know better than before what it is we are.' Dennis Potter, *The Listener*, 2 July 1987, p. 18.

My memory also contains my feelings, not in the same way as they are present to the mind when it experiences them, but in a quite different way that is in keeping with the special powers of the memory. For even when I am unhappy I can remember times when I was cheerful ... I can recall past fears and yet not feel afraid, and when I remember that I once wanted something, I can do so without wishing to have it now.[11]

He also considers the semantic relation between the two words *cogito* (I think) and *cogo* (I gather or collect) and comes to the conclusion that to think is to do more than speculate abstractly, for thoughts cannot leap unbidden to the brain to arrange themselves in logical argument, they must be connected to the past, past sensations, past emotions, past thoughts recalled and gathered into a pattern by an act of the memory.[12]

In the seventeenth section comes the crucial identification of memory and personality:

The power of the memory is great, O Lord. It is awe-inspiring in its profound and incalculable complexity. Yet it is my mind: it is my self.

But he promptly shrinks back from this bold identification as though he were fearful of its implications:

What then, am I, my God? What is my nature? A life that is ever varying, full of change, and of immense power.

There follows a slight digression, but having announced the possibility that the human being is what the human being remembers he returns to it, though more vaguely, at the end of the paragraph

This is the power of memory! This is the great force of life in living man, mental though he is![13]

Augustine has, here, anticipated the fundamental premise of twentieth century psycho-analysis: that the subconscious retains the imprint of every occurrence and emotion in a human life; that nothing is ever forgotten but is stored away in the memory and can, with whatever difficulty be brought out; that the process of the curing of neurosis begins with the eliciting of recollections of experiences from the past which the patient had believed he had forgotten but, in fact, had only suppressed. 'For we do not entirely

[11] *Confessions*, Book X, ch. 14.
[12] Ibid., Book X, ch. 11.
[13] Ibid., Book X, ch. 17.

forget what we remember that we have forgotten', Augustine writes, 'If we had completely forgotten it, we should not even be able to look for what was lost.'[14] It is a short step to the acknowledgement that the recollection of the past confers meaning in the present and, as in Proust, identity to the person remembering. Memory and personhood are co-terminous, hence the necessity for the subject to tell his own story. The ostensible motive for Augustine's writing of the *Confessions* was the ethical one: the encouragement of his readers in their struggle to live the Christian life; but might not the real, though unacknowledged, motive have been the 'achievement' of his own personality? Like Proust who has to relate the middle-aged Parisian Marcel to the Marcel who was a child in Combray, the Marcel who was an adolescent in Balbec, and the Marcel who was obsessed with Albertine; so Augustine has to integrate the various Augustines of the past (the Manichee, the neo-Platonist, the youth of powerful sexual energy and emotion) with the man who finds himself Bishop of Hippo. And it is only memory that can be used for this function: without memory the person cannot exist. The anthropology worked out in this tenth book: the perception of the purpose of the act of remembering and the power the memory has for conferring identity was to have profound implications for the whole of Western European culture and, more immediately, for Augustine's own theology. Decades later when he came to expound the doctrine of the Trinity the source of his analogies was the anthropology (more precisely the psychology) of this tenth book of the *Confessions*.'[15]

---

[14] Ibid., Book X, ch. 19.
[15] Those theologians, particularly of Eastern orthodoxy, who sometimes, quite correctly accuse Augustine's Trinitarian theology of being 'impersonal', also overlook the theory of personality which he was constructing in the *Confessions*. He specifically denies in *De Trinitate* that he believes in a God who has three modes of being participating in a kind of prior substance. By his analogies, of which by far the most important is the analogy of Memory, Understanding and Will, he tries to demonstrate what he believes to be true and what he knows his Eastern contemporaries have been teaching i.e. that the First Person (the Father) is the source of divinity in the Godhead and that this source is personal. He can call this First Person *Memoria* because the memory in his anthropology constitutes the person. Admittedly, it could be said that it is the ego who is doing the remembering; nonetheless, as we have seen, the ego who remembers and that which is remembered are inseparable if not identical, for the ego can only be the ego while it is remembering and in that activity personality resides.

In the structure of the work as a whole the book is the bridge by which the author crosses from the autobiographical to the theological mode. What follows are three long meditations on the first chapter of *Genesis*. They contain one of Augustine's most important contributions to the theology of the Western church: his exposition of the doctrine of creation. What becomes clearer with every reading of these books is that their originality and profundity are rooted in the theory of memory which has been developed in the transitional tenth book. His first concern is the idea of time, and in the eighteenth section of the eleventh book he considers the perplexing question of the 'existence' of the past and the future. Initially he concludes, as many others before him and many others after him have concluded, that only the present can be said to 'exist' and be 'real'.[16] But he cannot rest satisfied with that conclusion; he knows that the past — events, actions, sensations, feelings, thoughts — has a kind of existence, for the simple reason that he remembers it. Though the 'things' themselves as they were when they occurred have vanished, by the strange alchemy of memory they re-appear changed and re-located.

> My own childhood, which no longer exists, is in past time, which also no longer exists. But when I remember these days and describe them, it is in the present that I picture them to myself, because their picture is still present in my memory.[17]

The strange possibility presents itself that the only thing that *is* real is the memory. Considered from the perspective of time passing, no process can have meaning, nothing can be known, until it is completed and thus remembered from the standpoint of the end of time. The astonishing closing chapters (27-31) make this point over and over again.

These meditations on memory and time prepare the reader for Augustine's exposition of the doctrine of creation in the twelfth and thirteenth books. In many ways he does nothing more than elaborate, in his highly-charged, imaginative way, on what he has already received as orthodox teaching; but in so far as he constructs what might be called a psychological theory of time and creativity[18] he is building something new, and its foundations are his own theory of the person as presented in the tenth book. In this, as in his exposition of the doctrine of the Trinity, he parts company with his older contemporaries of the Eastern theological

---

[16] *Confessions*, Book XI, ch. 18.
[17] Ibid.
[18] Ibid., Book XII, ch. 29.

tradition *viz.* the Cappodocian Fathers. Gerhard Ladner in his essay, 'The Philosophical Anthropology of Gregory of Nyssa' points to the contrast between Augustine and Gregory when he remarks that 'Gregory's theory of time is closely bound up with his anthropology, [as Augustine's] in spite of the fact that, contrary to St Augustine's his concept of time is basically cosmological rather than psychological'.[19] The cosmological and the psychological. Is it far-fetched to see this contrast as an underlying and persistent theme in the centuries since Gregory and Augustine during which Eastern and Western theologians have confronted and often misunderstood one another?

---

[19] *Images and Ideas in the Middle Ages*, p. 855. See also Ladner's remarks on Augustine's concept of memory in *Augustine's Conception of the Reformation of Man*. Same volume pp. 595-608.

Bibliography
Augustine. *Confessions*. Translated and with an Introduction by R. S. Pine-Coffin. Penguin Books. 1961.

Ladner, Gerhard. *Images and Ideas in the Middle Ages. Selected Studies in History and Art*. Vol. II. Edizione di Storia e Litteratura. Roma. 1983.

Illingworth, J. R. *Personality. Human and Divine*. Macmillan & Co. 1894.

West, Rebecca. *Rebecca West. A Celebration*. Penguin Books. 1978.

Zizioulas, J. D. *Being as Communion Studies in Personhood and the Church*. D. L. T. 1985.

2. Christ's Humanity and Ours: John Owen

Alan Spence

I. In search of the truly human

The Christian tradition has generally regarded man in his being, behaviour and relationships as one who consistently falls short of his own highest possibilities and potential or, in more theological terminology, as one who has marred the divine image in which he was created. Consequently, there is a sense in which the lives of men and women, in their present state, are often considered as being something less than fully human, however paradoxical that may sound. Where then, we might ask, is an example to be found of the true nature of man, a paradigm of what he could and should be?

For much of its history the Church ascribed this normative status to man as he lived in a state of innocence before he turned away from God. If his nature has now been corrupted, it was argued, man's true being must be that which he had in his original, 'unfallen' condition. One consequence of such an emphasis was the development of detailed and often rather speculative views of unfallen man as an almost 'super-human' figure physically, mentally and spiritually.

The alternative is to consider the person of Jesus Christ as providing the paradigm of that which is truly human. Such an idea has far-reaching implications for a Christian understanding of man. If in Christ's person there has indeed been an historical substantiation of true humanity we have in his life among us both a plumbline by which to form an estimate of our present human condition and also the prototype of our destiny in God's redemptive purposes. Instead of interpreting our present being or condition in its relation to that of an ideal state in our prehistory, it is conceived in terms of its relation to the person of Christ and our new being in him, as we are created afresh in his likeness. The doctrine of a fall from primordial perfection thus becomes less significant for a Christian estimate of man than the doctrine of our regeneration in Christ and conformity to the divine image.

74

Why, then, has this apparently fruitful concept been so often neglected or undeveloped in the anthropological reflection of the Church? Why were theologians in the past led rather to speculate on the unfallen nature of Adam and why is so much present Christian anthropology quite unrelated to the human history of Jesus?

The difficulty seems to lie in an inability to conceive of the incarnate Christ as 'normative man'. Although those who hold to his divine sonship are usually quick to affirm his true humanity, there has, nevertheless, been in the past an unwillingness to give due weight to the Gospel testimony to his growth in grace, wisdom and knowledge; to his continual need of divine comfort and empowering through the Holy Spirit; and consequently to the implication that as man he stood just as we do, a creature totally dependent on his God. Modern theology has been far more ready to acknowledge that these things must be true of the humanity of Christ, but in divorcing the 'Christ of faith' from the 'historical Jesus', his human life with its religious, ethical, social and political dimensions has too often been treated as theologically insignificant and its anthropological implications neglected. Conversely, when Jesus' human history is taken seriously, a framework is seldom provided which is able to do full justice to the New Testament witness to his divine sonship and consequently to his universal significance.

In short, a survey of the history of doctrine suggests that the Church has by and large failed to bring its perception of Christ as the incarnation of the eternal Son of God into a coherent relation to the Gospel portrayal of Jesus as a man of the same nature as ourselves who is inspired by the Holy Spirit. Such a failure, I would argue, has resulted in the widespread neglect in practice of a foundation of Christian anthropology, that is, the doctrine that in the life of the incarnate Christ there has indeed been an historical exemplification of 'true man'. If we are to defend that foundation we will need to look more carefully at what is entailed by the ascription of full humanity to Jesus Christ.

II. John Owen and the humanity of Christ

The Puritan divine, John Owen, while vigorously defending the doctrine that Christ was the incarnation of the divine Son of God, nevertheless regarded his life as man among us as the prototype of Christian existence, and as continually empowered, comforted and sanctified by the Holy Spirit. He argued that the eternal Son of God assumed human nature into personal union with himself,

but, and this was the distinctive insight of his christology, he held
that all direct divine activity on that assumed human nature was
that of the Holy Spirit.

The question of interest to us is whether such a thesis is
justifiable. Other than in the actual assumption of human nature,
is it proper to conceive of the Spirit, rather than the Word, as the
divine agent acting directly on the humanity of Christ? Owen is
quite aware of the difficulties confronting his theory.

> It may, therefore, be, and it is objected, "That whereas the
> human nature of Christ is assigned as the immediate object of
> these operations of the Holy Ghost, and that nature was
> immediately, inseparably, and undividedly united unto the
> person of the Son of God, there doth not seem to be any need, nor
> indeed room, for any such operations of the Spirit; for could not
> the Son of God himself, in his own person, perform all things
> requisite both for the forming, supporting, sanctifying, and
> preserving of his own nature, without the especial assistance of
> the Holy Ghost?"[1]

Yet, in spite of these objections, Owen realised that it was
necessary to take seriously the Biblical portrait of Jesus as a man
anointed by the Holy Spirit, and was able to produce extensive
testimony from the Scriptures that throughout his life it was the
Spirit that formed, energised, sanctified, comforted, raised and
glorified the man Christ Jesus. The corollary, however, is not so
clear. Was Owen justified in holding that, other than in assuming
it to himself, the eternal Son in his divinity did not act directly or
immediately on his own human nature, but only indirectly through
his Spirit? Owen realised that to establish his position there was
a need to argue by the 'analogy of faith', that is from other
theological truths which bear upon it.[2]

In evaluating the validity of his theory, then, let us begin by
considering the christological difficulties involved in maintaining
its converse, that is, that the divine Word or eternal Son determines
the human life of Jesus directly or immediately, rather than
indirectly by means of his Spirit.

---

[1] John Owen, *A Discourse Concerning the Holy Spirit. The Works of
John Owen*, 16 volumes (vols. I-XVI of the 1850-53 edition), Ed. by
W.H.Goold, The Banner of Truth Trust (London, 1972), first edition
1674, vol.3, p. 160.

[2] *Works 3*, p. 160.

III. The Apollinarian solution

The Arian debate focused attention on the status of the Word or
Son of God. At the Council of Nicea it was acknowledged that he
was of one substance with the Father and this was eventually
recognised as a standard of christological orthodoxy. But long
before the dust was to settle on that discussion the question of
the Word's relation to what we here will simply call the humanity
of Jesus began to surface. Athanasius outlines his understanding
of it.

> Now, the Word of God in His man's nature was not like that (of
> the human soul limited to the body); for He was not bound to his
> body, but rather was himself wielding it, so that He was not
> only in it, but was actually in everything, and while external to
> the universe abode in the Father only.[3]

Two or three ideas typical of Athanasius's christology are suggested
here and it might be helpful to highlight them. The Logos or Word
is the personal governing principle which provides and gives life
to the whole of creation and his action with respect to his human
nature is one aspect of this wider work, similar in some respects
to that of the soul to the body. In fact, Athanasius often refers to
the body as the instrument of the Word which he here graphically
portrays as being wielded by him. In all this the agent of Jesus'
human nature is clearly the Word, while his humanity is merely
the instrument through which he acts. Kelly aptly describes this
relation: "...the Word for Athanasius was the governing principle,
or *hegemonikon*, in Jesus Christ, the subject of all the sayings,
experiences and actions attributed to the Gospel figure."[4]
However, with such an uncompromising conception of the
eternal Son's determination of Jesus' life, some explanation was
needed to account for the human frailties and sufferings which the
Gospels attribute to him. Athanasius does so by simply ascribing
all these to his flesh.

> ...in nature the Word Himself is impassible, and yet because
> of that flesh which he put on, these things are ascribed to Him,
> since they are proper to the flesh, and the body itself is proper
> to the Saviour.[5]

---

[3] Athanasius, *Incarnation of the Word*, NPNF, second series, vol.IV, 17,
p.45.
[4] J. N. D. Kelly, *Early Christian Doctrines*, fifth edition, Adam &
Charles Black (London, 1977), pp. 285ff.
[5] Athanasius, *Four Discourses Against the Arians*, III 34, NPNF, second
series, vol. IV, p. 412.

Some things then are spoken of him as God and others of him as 'He that bore flesh'. Athanasius suggests it is a fairly straight-forward matter to distinguish between these two areas. "For if we recognise what is proper to each, and see and understand that both these things and those are done by One, we are right in our faith, and shall never stray."[6]

This explanation does not fit as awkwardly with his original position as it might first appear, particularly if we remember that Athanasius viewed the relation of the Word to the humanity as similar to the Platonic and therefore dualistic understanding of the relation of soul and body. We simply have to recognise what belongs to each. The difficulty, however, arises when we consider Christ's frailties, not merely in his physical body or in his emotions, but in his intellect, will and spirituality. Athanasius' model will not allow him to ascribe these to the flesh for these are functions not of the instrument but of him who wields it. He is, therefore, forced to be less than fair with the passages in Scripture which speak of Jesus growing in wisdom and grace or lacking complete knowledge.[7]

This brief analysis of Athanasius' christology is instructive in that it highlights the inherent difficulty faced by any theory which would emphasise the Word's role in directly determining the humanity of Jesus. For if the Word is the governing principle of his life, what account are we to give of the human will, knowledge and spirituality of Jesus?

Apollinarius' answer was unambiguous: the Word in effect replaced these faculties in the life of Jesus. We would be unwise, however, to view this as merely a naive short-circuit of the christological problem. His handling of the issues was both sensitive and subtle. For soteriological reasons he was whole-heartedly opposed to the dualism suggested by any view that there were two principles operating in Christ. "The metaphysical framework from which Apollinarius (sought) to interpret the being of Christ (was) a picture of the substantial unity of man as a synthesis of body and soul."[8] He understood the Logos to be both the directive principle of Christ's life and the life-giving energy of his whole physical being, resulting in one vital hypostasis or nature.

---

[6] Athanasius, III 35, p. 413.
[7] Athanasius, III 51, pp. 421ff.
[8] Aloys Grillmeier, *Christ in Christian Tradition, vol. I, From the Apostolic Age to Chalcedon* (451), E.T. by John Bowden, second edition, Mowbrays (London & Oxford, 1975), pp. 330ff.

Apollinarius was both carefully and logically developing a tendency that was already present in Athanasius and other supporters of the Nicene Creed. But when what was implied by them became explicit in his writing and when a human mind was not simply neglected, but actually denied of Jesus, the Church reacted strongly. At the Council of Constantinople it was generally accepted that the manhood of Christ must be complete, a whole man with his own human mind or soul.

Historical theologians have described Athanasius' form of christology as being of the Word-flesh type in contrast to the Word-man type which emphasised that Christ's humanity possessed a mind or rational soul. Although this characterisation is open to the dangers inherent in any such over-simplification it does focus attention on one of the chief reasons the latter form triumphed in the christological debate and that was its ability to satisfy more adequately the demands of soteriology. The widely accepted theory of the atonement at that time recognised the Son's assumption of human nature to be a means by which God renewed man's nature in general. Gregory Nazianzen's celebrated expression summarises the argument:

> For that which He has not assumed He has not healed; but that which is united to his Godhead is also saved.[9]

Clearly if the mind of man, which is the seat of impurity in him, is to be saved, it is essential that the human nature which Christ assumed should include a fully human mind.

Our interest in this discussion is with the functional relation between the Word or divine nature and the humanity o f Jesus. In the fourth century the emphasis on the Word's immediate or direct determination of the human life of Christ inclined naturally towards Apollinarianism. However, the Church's reaction to this theory and its affirmation that Christ possessed a human mind did not mean that the Word was no longer considered as immediately determining the human life of Jesus. The 'communicatio idiomatum', although originally put forward as a linguistic explanation for the practice of referring the action of one nature to the other, soon developed into a way of conceiving how the human nature was effectively and directly determined by the divine. Thus John of Damascus writes with respect to Christ's human will:

> And we hold that it is just the same with the deification of the will; for its natural activity was not changed but united with his

---

[9] Gregory Nazianzen, *To Cledonius the Priest against Apollinarius*, ep. CI, NPNF, second series, vol. VII, p. 440.

divine and omnipotent will, and became the will of God, made man.[10]

The result was that orthodox theology particularly in the East, although affirming that Christ was ontologically one with us lacking nothing that was human, yet implicitly denied that his human nature thought, learned and responded to God in a way that was continuous with our own. Almost without exception the Fathers would not concede that Jesus grew in knowledge or needed to pray for grace for himself. If the Word determines the humanity, acting directly upon it, the full functioning of the human nature is effectively denied. I believe C. E. Raven was by and large correct in his assessment: "Apollinarius can only be condemned by those who are prepared to allow that the whole Greek school from Justin to Leontius and John of Damascus is similar ... since the divergences between them and the heresiarch are merely verbal and superficial."[11]

So far our discussion has been limited to the Patristic Age, but some of the same patterns are apparent in the christology of more modern times. As interest grew in the concept of man's personality in the eighteenth and nineteenth centuries, its 'core' was often understood as the centre from which his 'authentic' actions sprang. With this came a new form of Apollinarianism. The core of Christ's 'personality', his ego, was understood to lie in the divine Son rather than in his human nature and in this way the Word was conceived as the immediate determinative force in the 'personal' dimensions of Jesus' human actions. So Maurice Relton argued:

> The Divine Logos was capable of being the Ego, not only of his Divine but also of His human nature; because His Personality in virtue of its Divinity already embraced all that is most distinctive of a truly human personality.[12]

---

[10] John of Damascus, *Exposition of the Orthodox Faith*, III 17, NPNF, second series, vol. IX, p.66.

[11] Quoted in Harry Johnson, *The Humanity of the Saviour. A Biblical and Historical Study of the Human Nature of Christ in relation to Original Sin, with special reference to its Soteriological Significance*, The Epworth Press (London, 1962), p. 196.

[12] H. Maurice Relton, *A Study in Christology. The Problem of the Relation of the Two Natures in the Person of Christ*, SPCK (London, 1934), p. 227. P. T. Forsyth in his important book *The Person and Place of Jesus Christ* (London, 1909) develops this idea. "But if we follow the New Testament as a whole and as a Gospel, we must think of the divine element as constituting the historic personality ..." p.247.

The theory found apparent support in a misunderstanding of the earlier theory of 'enhypostasia', conceiving of it in psychological rather than ontological terms, and possibly it was this that prevented many from seeing its more natural link with Apollinarius' position.

Quite different in content but encouraged by a similar impulse has been the concept of the 'kenosis' of the Son in the incarnation, when this has been understood as his self-emptying or laying aside of aspects of his divine nature. With the underlying assumption that the eternal Son must directly determine the human life, yet unwilling to divinise Jesus' human actions, theologians have found it necessary to argue that there is some voluntary limitation on the Son's divine attributes. Although the theory has come under widespread criticism, more subtle mutations of it continue to appear, for those who would uphold the doctrine of the incarnation see no other way for the Son to determine and yet not violate Jesus' humanity, even though this be at the heavy theological cost of 'humanising' the divine nature.

IV. An alternative account

It would seem, then, that there are inherent difficulties in any theory based on the assumption that the Son directly determines the human nature of Christ. But is this the only alternative? As Gregory of Nyssa put before the adherents of Apollinarianism:

> Was it necessarily the case . . . that two complete entities, divinity and humanity, could not coalesce so as to form a real unity? Or that the coexistence of two distinct volitional principles in one individual was inconceivable? [13]

In short, are we left with the unsatisfactory choice of the divinisation of man, or the 'humanisation' of God, in order to explain the incarnation, or can we overturn the assumption that the Son directly determines the human nature and allow rather that each nature operates according to its own characteristic properties, finding its unity in the one incarnate 'hypostasis' or person, so that the actions performed in each nature are in fact the actions of the one person Jesus Christ? Leo in his celebrated 'Tome' indicates his favour for this latter alternative:

> For each nature retains its own distinctive character without loss; and as the form of God does not take away the form of a

[13] Quoted in Kelly, p.296.

servant, so the form of a servant does not diminish the form of God.... Each form, in communion with the other, performs the function that is proper to it; that is, the Word performing what belongs to the Word, and the flesh carrying on what belongs to the flesh.[14]

And this in essence was the position maintained in the Definition of Chalcedon:

... the distinction of natures being in no way abolished because of the union, but rather the characteristic property of each nature being preserved, and concurring into one Person and one subsistence ...[15]

A common error, I believe, in reading the Definition is to interpret its reference to the two natures statically rather than dynamically, that is, to see it as maintaining that Christ had a full complement of human properties, but that these did not necessarily operate in a human way. But what does it mean to affirm that Christ has a human will other than that he willed as a human? By 'the characteristic property of each nature being preserved', those who formulated the Definition surely intended to summarise the concept which has been more fully expressed by Leo in the phrase 'each form in communion with the other performs the function that is proper to it'. If this is so, a framework was given in the Definition of Chalcedon which allowed the humanity of Christ to be conceived as effective, operating according to its own characteristic principles rather than as directly determined by the Word.

We have argued that the Church did not in practice hold on to this insight, for its soteriology required only the existence rather than the full operation of a human mind or rational soul. The consequent development of the concept of *communicatio idiomatum* allowed this human mind and spirituality of Christ to be understood as so determined by the divine nature that a true appreciation of Christ's humanity was effectively lost.

In the seventeenth century John Owen reaffirmed the concept of Christ's human nature as 'autokineton', that is as a self-determining spiritual principle, fully self-conscious and as creature open and responsive to God, rather than as immediately or directly determined by the Son. He held that:

---

[14] *Quoted in Creeds, Councils and Controversies. Documents illustrative of the history of the Church A.D. 337-461*, Ed. by J.Stevenson, SPCK (London, 1966), p.319.
[15] Stevenson, p.337.

His divine nature was not unto him in the place of a soul, nor did immediately operate the things which he performed, as some of old vainly imagined; but being a perfect man, his rational soul was in him the immediate principle of all his moral operations, even as ours are in us.[16]

His christology, along with that of Chalcedon, thus forms part of what we have described as an alternative account of the relation of the divine and human natures in Christ. But how are we to assess its validity?

V. The nature of Christ's humanity

It would appear from our above discussion that the argument for the Word's determination of the human nature of Christ resolves itself into a question concerning the reality of his humanity. The real point at issue is whether the experiences of the man Christ Jesus were continuous with our own. Did he pray, face temptation, depend on divine strength and encouragement, grow in knowledge and grace and struggle to live a life of obedience in a way which was not qualitatively different from the possibilities that are open to us? In short, did he as man face God as we do? If he did it would appear that his human nature is not directly determined by his divinity, but has its own principle or centre of operation, experiencing and knowing God through the Spirit.

What arguments can Owen bring to bear to establish that Christ's humanity was indeed of this sort? We will consider two aspects of his soteriology before examining his interpretation of Jesus as God's revelation.

a. Jesus as our prototype
Owen understood man's alienation from God as arising from his defacement of the divine image which he bore. This image included his moral likeness to God in righteousness and holiness; his ability to recognise and respond to God's glory in creation and also the power to obey him and thereby to live continually with him in a relation of love and trust.[17] A necessary aspect of his reconciliation to God, therefore, is the restoration to his nature of this lost image.

---

[16] *Works 3*, p.169.
[17] John Owen, *Christologia: Or, a Declaration of the Glorious Mystery of the Person of Christ, Works*, vol.1, pp.182ff.

How are we to understand Christ's part in bringing about this renewal of God's image among men? Of particular significance to our present discussion is the passive role that Owen ascribed to Christ in this work, arguing that the divine image was first renewed in Christ's human nature, as a prototype of what God by his Spirit was to do in the whole Church. God's purpose, he held, is that Christ:

> ... might be the pattern and example of the renovation of the image of God in us, and of the glory that doth ensue thereon. He is in the eye of God as the idea of what he intends in us ... [18]

This is an important concept and we need to pause and consider how well founded it is. It receives its impetus from his perception that the Christian life can be understood in terms of conformity to the person of Christ and that the Spirit is given to us for no other purpose than to unite us to him and make us like him.[19]

> The great design of God in his grace is, that as we have borne the "image of the first Adam" in the depravation of our natures, so we should bear the "image of the second" in their renovation.[20]

Clearly there is widespread Biblical support for the idea that our spiritual renewal and growth in grace can be described in terms of our conformity to Christ.

> And we all, with unveiled face, beholding the glory of the Lord, are being changed into his likeness from one degree of glory to another; for this comes from the Lord who is the Spirit (2 Cor 3.18).

Now Owen held that this transformation of the Christian into the likeness of Christ is in effect the restoration of the divine image in him. Such an identification was possible because of his interpretation of the divine image in terms of sanctification and of spiritual life. The Christian is therefore called to conformity to Christ or equivalently to put on a new nature created after the likeness or image of God (cf Eph 4.23). They are in essence the same thing.

Owen appears to be justified, then, in holding that Christ is the prime example for the Christian life and that assimilation to his likeness is to be identified with the renewal of the divine image in the believer. But has he any grounds for arguing that this divine

---

[18] *Works 1*, p.170.
[19] *Works 1*, p.172.
[20] *Works 1*, p.171.

image was first restored in Christ's own human nature so that his whole life was in effect the prototype of the Christian life? A passage which he finds particularly instructive in this matter is from the second chapter of Hebrews.

> For it was fitting that he, for whom and by whom all things exist, in bringing many sons to glory, should make the pioneer of their salvation perfect through suffering. For he who sanctifies and those who are sanctified have all one origin. That is why he is not ashamed to call them brethren ... (Heb 2.10,11, RSV).

A sanctifying work is presupposed in Christ who thereby becomes a pioneer in the faith for other believers. As Owen argues: "It is Christ who sanctifieth believers; yet it is from God, who first sanctified him, that he and they might be of one, and so become brethren, as bearing the image of the same Father."[21] What God did in Christ he was later to do in us, and thus the source of our sanctification is common, the image we bear is common, thus we are truly brethren.

We have spent some time considering this concept of Christ as the prototype of the believer because it clearly has far-reaching implications for an understanding of his humanity. The man Christ Jesus as the object of the Spirit's sanctifying and renewing work must have learnt and experienced grace as we do, knowing sanctification through suffering and finding God's help through fervent prayer. If he is truly our prototype and example then he too must have stood before God "in a genuinely human attitude of adoration, obedience, a most radical sense of creaturehood."[22]

We are examining whether Owen can establish that Christ's humanity was such that his experience of God was in no way qualitatively different from possibilities that are open to us. So far we have looked at the implications which arise from his understanding of Christ's passive role as the prototype of the Christian life. Let us now examine what may be learnt of his humanity from Owen's exposition of the active part Christ played in giving over his life to suffering and death.

b. Jesus as a willing priest
Owen believed Christ's work as Mediator between man and God could be referred to three distinct offices or roles which he

---

[21] *Works* 1, p.171.

[22] Karl Rahner, *Theological Investigations*, vol. I, E.T. by Cornelius Ernst, Helicon Press (Baltimore, 1961), Darton, Longman & Todd (London, 1961), pp.157ff.

exercised with respect to the Church. As king he received a delegated authority from God to rule his subjects and to subdue his enemies. As prophet he was raised up by God from among his brethren to make known to the Church the divine will by teaching and instruction. But his office as priest, whereby he made atonement for his people, differs from the other two in that it is directed not towards men but towards God on behalf of men.[23]

God is, therefore, the object of Christ's priestly work. It is before him that Christ stands as our advocate and continues to make intercession on our behalf; and it is to God that he offered himself as a sacrifice. For the high priest is always chosen from among men to act on their behalf in relation to God, to offer gifts and sacrifices for sins (cf Heb 5.1). This means that although salvation should be considered, from first to last, as God's gracious and loving initiative in reconciling an alienated and helpless world, nevertheless, the actual act of atonement must also be seen as an act towards God of one who is man. We will consider the nature of this act and its implications for Christ's humanity by briefly following one line of Owen's discussion.

He held that there was no value or efficacy in the sufferings and death of Christ considered in themselves:

> For what excellency of the nature of God could have been demonstrated in the penal sufferings of one absolutely and in all respects innocent . . . ?[24]

Its effectiveness can only be understood with respect to God's covenant to save sinful men, and it is in this context alone that these sufferings are made good and tend to God's glory. Similarly the efficacy of the sacrifice is related to the attitude of the offerer:

> It is the mind, and not the matter, that gives measure and acceptance unto an offering.[25]

Owen wished to emphasise that it is Christ's manner and motivation in the giving over of his life that brings glory to God and value to his sacrifice. This motivation included his love to mankind and compassion to those caught in sin; his unspeakable zeal for the glory of God; his attitude of submission and obedience to his will; and his own faith and trust in God.[26]

[23] John Owen, *An Exposition of the Epistle to the Hebrews*, 7 volumes (vols. XVIII-XXIV of the 1855 edition), Ed. by W. H. Goold, reprinted by Baker Book House (Grand Rapids, Michigan, 1980), vol.2, p.149.
[24] *Hebrews 2*, p.89.
[25] *Hebrews 2*, p.155.
[26] *Works 3*, pp.177-179.

But by recognising that Christ's attitude in laying down his life is an integral part of the efficacy of his death, Owen effectively undermines what we might call an Apollinarian view of the atonement. For if it does not merely consist in his physical death, but in the fear and the tears, in the faith and the prayer and in the submission of the will that led to it, then an active human mind and will are an essential aspect of that whole event. To substantiate his argument let us consider his exposition of the following passage from Hebrews:

> In the days of his flesh, Jesus offered up prayers and supplications, with loud cries and tears, to him who was able to save him from death, and he was heard for his godly fear. (Heb.5.7)

Owen holds that 'flesh' is used here to signify the frailties, weakness and infirmities of our nature in which Christ shared throughout his life, but which here refers particularly to his last days when all his sorrows, trials and temptations came to a head. The preceding verses show that the prayers and supplications he offered at this time were an aspect of his priestly ministry. They should not be considered as 'petitory' to procure that which is good, but as 'deprecatory' to keep off or turn away that which is evil, as were those of the high priest when he confessed the sins of Israel over the head of the scape-goat in order that the curse of the law might be averted."[27]

But the priest is in sympathy with those for whom he prays, for he too is beset with weakness. Owen, therefore, understands the verse as referring directly to Jesus' agony in prayer at Gethsemane, and he argues that the torment experienced there can not be explained merely as the fear of a man facing a gruesome death. "Where, then, is the glory of his spiritual strength and fortitude? where the beauty of the example which herein he set before us?"[28] We must, rather, look for a deeper cause for the dreadful, trembling conflict which seemed almost to dissolve his whole being.

Owen believed it had to do with Jesus' awareness of God in his holiness and righteousness as the author and upholder of the law and his understanding of his own impending death in terms of the law's curse (Gal.3.13). It is this that caused his sense of spiritual desertion and separation from all comfort and joy in his relation with God the Father, and which culminated in his cry of dereliction from the cross.[29]

---

[27] *Hebrews 4*, pp.496ff.
[28] *Hebrews 4*, p.503.
[29] *Hebrews 4*, pp.506ff.

The inadequacy of any portrayal of Christ's passion as the suffering of God at the hands of men, or the identification of God with man's tragic condition, now becomes apparent. Gethsemane does not allow Christ's tribulations to be viewed so docetically. The central actor in that dark drama experiences spiritual separation from God and he does so with human fears and a human faith. The person of Christ is truly God and thereby value, dignity and efficacy was given to his passion, nevertheless it was in his human nature that he gave himself up, knew the agony of spiritual dereliction and tasted death.

Owen's theology is interesting because in it there is recovered an appreciation of the full and active humanity of Christ. His exposition of Christ as a willing priest who lays down his life as an atonement for sin requires an understanding of his humanity as one which knew the full depths of spiritual desertion and dereliction by God. Yet if he was both man and God how could his humanity experience such a sense of separation from God? Owen answers:

> And this dereliction was possible, and proceeded from hence, in that all communications from the divine nature unto the human, beyond subsistence, were voluntary.[30]

We are back where we began. The eternal Son does not immediately determine the humanity of Christ, the communication is 'voluntary' rather than 'natural' and is always through the Holy Spirit. A sense of divine desertion is possible for Christ as man in his suffering precisely because his experience of God is not immediate but is indirect and by means of the Spirit.

We have been examining the validity of Owen's assertion that the eternal Son does not directly determine or operate on the human life of Jesus. On the one hand we have argued that its converse tended historically towards some form of either Apollinarianism or kenoticism. On the other we have seen how Owen's soteriology requires a view of Christ's humanity as operating according to its own principles, rather than as directly determined by the Word. His soteriology thereby provides positive support for his theory. There is, however, an idea in contemporary theology which appears to undermine it radically. This is the conception of Christ as God's self-revelation, which was developed by Karl Barth. Bet us briefly consider how damaging it actually is to Owen's position.

c. *Jesus as God's revelation*
The point at issue is whether Jesus Christ reveals God by his own

---

[30] *Hebrews 4*, p.507.

divine nature or through his hum-anity as it is inspired by the Holy Spirit. The former is destructive of Owen's theory for it implies that in revealing God, Christ's divine nature is the direct determining principle of his words and actions. This is the position that Barth affirms:

> ... the statement about Christ's deity is to be understood in the sense that Christ reveals his Father. But this Father of His is God. He who reveals Him, then reveals God. But who can reveal God except God Himself?[31]

The underlying concept is that revelation must be self-revelation and therefore only the divine nature can truly reveal God. In fact Christ's deity is conceived in terms of his revelation of God. Pannenberg is aware of the importance of this argument and maintains that: "The demonstration of the connection of Jesus' divinity with the concept of revelation constitutes one of Barth's greatest theological contributions."[32] I believe its significance in the world of religious ideas lies in the fact that it gave to the post-Enlightenment Church a way of conceiving the deity of Christ which did not appear to suffer from the epistemological problems that had discredited the naive objectivism of an earlier age.

Owen's understanding of Christ in terms of God's revelation is quite different as is apparent from his discussion of the opening verses of Hebrews:

> In the past God spoke to our forefathers through the prophets at many times and in various ways, but in the last days he has spoken to us by his Son (Heb 1.1).

There is both a distinction and a measure of continuity between the revelation that came through the prophets and that which was in Christ. The distinction has to do with the being and status of the person through whom the revelation is given and it is this that the author of the epistle goes on to develop at some length. The continuity arises from the fact that it is God who in both cases is the author of the revelation.[33]

---

[31] Karl Barth, *Church Dogmatics, vol.I, part one, The Doctrine of the Word of God*, second edition, Ed. by G. W. Bromiley & T. F. Torrance, T. & T. Clark (Edinburgh, 1980), p.406.

[32] Wolfhart Pannenberg, *Jesus — God and Man*, SCM Press (London, 1985), p.130.

[33] *Hebrews 3*, pp.5ff.

Owen examines the idea that it is the Father and not the Son who is the source of the revelation. It indicates that God has so revealed his mind to him so as to be said to speak to us in him. Owen sees it as a characteristic of the whole New Testament witness that it is from the Father that Christ heard the word and learnt the doctrine that he declared to the Church, it did not come from himself:

> And this is asserted wherever there is mention made of the Father's sending, sealing, anointing, commanding, teaching him, of his doing the will, speaking the words, seeking the glory, obeying the commands of him that sent him.[34]

Now if the source of the revelation is the Father, how then does he reveal himself to the Son? For in his divine nature Jesus Christ, "as he was the eternal Word and Wisdom of the Father . . . had an omnisciency of the whole nature and will of God, as the Father himself hath, because the same with that of the Father, their will and wisdom being the same."[35] It was clearly, then, not as the eternal Word that the Son was taught by the Father, but as he took the form of a servant.

> The Lord Jesus Christ discharged his office and work of revealing the will of the Father in and by his human nature . . . for although the person of Christ, God and man, was our mediator . . . yet his human nature was that wherein he discharged the duties of his office and the 'principium quod' of all his mediatory actings, 1 Tim 2.5.[36]

Therefore, as Christ received the Spirit that he might in all holiness obey God, so also was he endowed with the Spirit beyond measure that he might be "the great prophet of the church, in whom the Father would speak and give out the last revelation of himself."[37] What distinguishes the revelation in Christ from that of Moses and all other prophets is "the infinite excellency of his person above theirs."[38] The person of the mediator, God and man, as the agent of the revelation gives to it its dignity and value, even though it was done through his human nature.

It is apparent from this outline that if Barth's conception of revelation is in essence correct then Owen's interpretation of the relation of the divine nature to the humanity of Christ, and

[34] *Hebrews 3*, pp.28ff.
[35] *Hebrews 3*, p.30.
[36] *Hebrews 3*, p.30.
[37] *Hebrews 3*, p.30.
[38] *Hebrews 3*, p.31.

consequently his appreciation of the radical creatureliness of Christ in all his mediatorial work, is mistaken. Now it is rather unlikely that a major foundation of contemporary theology will be effectively discredited in the eye of the reader by these few paragraphs, nevertheless in defence of Owen's position we raise the following questions.

Firstly, how firm is the biblical foundation for the conception of revelation as self-revelation, that is, that only God can reveal God? Pannenberg who upholds the idea, recognises that it is modern. "The exclusive use of the concept of revelation for God's self-disclosure goes back to German Idealism, especially to Hegel."[39] He concedes that the words in Scripture translated by 'to reveal' and 'revelation' do not have this meaning at all, but believes that the content of the idea can be found in the Old Testament 'word of demonstration' formulas "that designate the knowledge of Yahweh's divinity as the purpose of God in history".[40]

Clearly the power of the idea lies not in its biblical base but in its ability to provide a framework for conceiving of the divinity of Christ in a post-Kantian world. How would Owen respond to so pragmatic a defence of its use? It is worthy of note that in the apologetics of his own day the divinity of Christ was often derived from the miraculous nature of his ministry. Owen, however, did not believe it was possible to do this.

> The naked working of miracles, I confess, without the influence of such other considerations as this argument is attended withal in relation to Jesus Christ, will not alone of itself assert a divine nature in him who is the instrument of their working or production.[41]

An important principle emerges. According to Owen it is not possible simply to read off Christ's divinity from his incarnate activity, whether it be his sinless life, miraculous ministry, supernatural birth, resurrection or, as in our above discussion, in his revelation of God. For although in his person he was both God and man, his work of mediation was carried out through his human nature. This meant there were no aspects of his activity where God, or the divine nature, replaced the normal operation of his humanity. In short if we reject Apollinarianism there is no element of Christ's incarnate life which we can simply isolate as being that of God and not of man.

---

[39] Pannenberg, p.127.
[40] Pannenberg, p.128.
[41] John Owen, *Vindiciae Evangelicae; or the Mystery of the Gospel Vindicated and Socinianism Examined. Works*, vol.12, p.174.

How then do we come to know the divinity of Christ? Owen held that it was by the Holy Spirit. It was the Spirit that bore witness to Christ "that he was the Son of God, the true Messiah, and that the work that he performed in the world was committed unto him by God the Father to accomplish".[42] Christ died an ignominious death and was believed by most to be an imposter. It was the Spirit's work by means of his small group of followers to testify of him through their words and through the signs which accompanied them and it is by him that faith is maintained in the world today.[43] It is the Spirit that convicts and reproves of sin, but it is also by him that the veil is lifted and we are able to see the glory of God in the face of Christ Jesus.

We have argued that whenever the divine nature is considered as directly determining the humanity of Christ, some aspect of his human nature is either neglected or denied. This leads us naturally to a second question. How does Barth in this context understand the relation between the Word of God, that is Christ as God's revelation, and his humanity?

> Is the *humanitas Christi* as such the revelation? Does the divine sonship of Jesus Christ mean that God's revealing has now been transmitted as it were to the existence of the man Jesus of Nazareth, that this has thus become identical with it?[44]

Barth goes on to show why the answer must be negative. Jesus Christ the man is not to be identified with the revelation. His argument makes sense once we accept his interpretation of the concept of revelation. Nevertheless the breach implied here between the Word of God and Jesus the man can only be damaging for christology for it inevitably leads to the neglect of the historical life of Christ as the basis for our knowledge of God. Thus Barth argues in his early writings:

> Jesus Christ is also in fact the Rabbi of Nazareth who is hard to know historically and whose work, when He is known, might seem to be a little commonplace compared to more than one of the other founders of religions and even compared to some of the later representatives of His own religion . . . . The veil is thick. We do not have the Word of God otherwise than in the mystery of its secularity. This means, however, that we have it in a form which as such is not the Word of God . . .[45]

---

[42] *Works 3*, pp.183ff
[43] *Works 3*, p.184.
[44] Karl Barth, I/1, p.323.
[45] Karl Barth, I/1, p.165.

With this Owen would have sharply disagreed. There is a suggestion in it that Jesus of Nazareth, the historical form of the Word of God, is secondary. We can be agnostic about the historical details of his life and relatively unimpressed by his person, nevertheless we are still called to offer worship and obedience to Jesus Christ as the transcendent Word of God. But Christ the Mediator is one person, not two. Our response to the Rabbi of Nazareth is our response to God's Son. Owen held that Jesus' historical life is commonplace only to those whose eyes have not been opened by the Spirit to recognise the glory of his person. The distinction lies in our perception, not in his reality. The humanity of his one person has ultimate significance, for in it and through it God is made known to us and redemption is won for us.

We have attempted to undermine Barth's interpretation of revelation as self-revelation by indicating the limited nature of its scriptural basis and also by suggesting some of the unhelpful implications it has for his christology, in so far as it was dependent on this model. (It is significant that in Barth's later work he, like the early church before him, began to emphasise the concept of sonship in favour of that of 'logos' or self-revelation as a more adequate way of understanding the person of Christ.) Our criticism of Barth's thesis is important to the argument of this paper for his conception of divine revelation as the action of Christ in his divinity does undermine Owen's theory that the eternal Son determines his human nature only indirectly and by means of the Holy Spirit. We believe, however, that Owen's position can and should be defended for it offers a coherent way of understanding the true creaturehood of the man Christ Jesus within an incarnational christology.

VI. The self-consciousness of Jesus

On the basis of Owen's theory it would appear that we are entitled to ask questions about the self-consciousness of Jesus as he is man. There might or there might not be sufficient material for New Testament scholars to provide responsible answers, but there does not seem to me to be any compelling argument why the venture is either intrinsically impious or doomed to failure. If the physical body of Christ operated as ours does, what ground, other than incipient Apollinarianism, can there be for maintaining that his human mind or self-understanding was wholly different from our own? Although Owen did not explicitly deal with Jesus' self-consciousness, he was interested in the extent of the knowledge possessed by the incarnate Christ and the manner by which he attained it.

In his commentary on Hebrews he argued that Christ had in principle a complete knowledge of God and his will. But in practice this was not his to exercise either as a child or as an adult, but rather he grew "in all that wisdom and knowledge which the human nature was capable of . . . without destroying its finite being or variety of conditions".[46] There seems no reason, then, to consider the functioning of Jesus' human self-consciousness as discontinuous with our own, forming and developing as he grew in his experience of himself, the world and of God. Rather, it was in the content of this perception of himself that the distinction lay. Of Jesus' self-understanding we offer a tentative description, for although we are uncertain of the details, we believe such an outline is in principle possible to draw.

Through his experience of God, mediated by the Spirit, Jesus came to believe that he was living in a unique relation to the God of Israel, analogous to that of a son to his father. Linked to this there was a growing conviction that he had been commissioned by God to a work of ultimate redemptive significance among his people. The Gospels suggest that this faith in his distinctive relation to the Father required divine support and strengthening, the outstanding example of which occurred at his baptism when a 'voice from heaven' affirmed his divine sonship. There were also times when this faith was tested and challenged and the accounts of his temptation in the wilderness give a dramatic description of his struggle and final refusal to seek some explicit and external evidence which would prove to himself the reality of his relation to God. Prayer was thus a spiritual necessity for his own faith and for the successful completion of his mission. Suffering proved to be the sensitive but effective divine instrument by which his person was refined and developed into spiritual maturity. P.T.Forsyth inquires:

> Is it too much to press into the deeper meaning and condition of such growing obedience, and to say that as he did the deeper will he knew the deeper doctrine, his *grasp* of sonship also grew?[47]

How much he knew and when he came to understand it is an ongoing task for New Testament scholarship to explore, as is the investigation of the part played by the various Old Testament messianic concepts in his perception of who he was. However, it seems to have been through the mediation of one or more of these

---

[46] *Hebrews 3*, p.28.
[47] Forsyth, *The Person and Place of Jesus Christ*, op. cit., p.121.

conceptions that he came to believe that he had a personal history that went back before time. This does not imply that he now had a universal knowledge of all reality, physical and spiritual, but rather that he identified himself with one who had been at the Father's side. It would be on the basis of this developed self-understanding that he found the personal authority to forgive men of their sins and offer them life in the kingdom which he taught was being inaugurated in and through his ministry. It would also have provided him a framework to understand the divine call or mission that led him finally to Jerusalem and death.

He was not suffering from religious delusion for the content of his self-understanding is known by the Church to be true, the person who argued in the streets of Jerusalem was not only a descendant of David, but he was also his Lord — an idea that appears to have delighted the common people although undoubtedly scandalising the religious leadership of the day (Mark 12.35-37). Neither was his experience that of a schizophrenic for the reason that the divine nature never suddenly 'broke in', leaving his human mind and will as a mere spectator of his actions. Rather, his human self-consciousness knew and experienced God always indirectly and by means of the Holy Spirit, for only in this way could it remain truly human.

Here lies our motivation for this excursion into the self-understanding of Jesus. If his knowledge of his own divine sonship flowed out of an active and tested faith, (and how else can we interpret the wilderness temptations?) and if his human self-understanding was an integrated and continuous reality, it would seem that Owen was correct in arguing that the divine nature determined the humanity of Christ only indirectly and voluntarily by means of the Holy Spirit, rather than immediately or naturally, in which case his thoughts and ideas would have been those of God.

VII. Conclusion

Our concern in this paper has been to defend the doctrine that Jesus Christ exemplifies the true nature of man, a doctrine which has suffered in the past from the reticence of an incarnational christology to concede in practice his full and active humanity. John Owen's ability to do so appears to have depended on his thesis that, other than in assuming it into personal subsistence with himself, the Son acted on his human nature only indirectly and by means of the Spirit. We have had to consider, therefore, whether such an apparently productive thesis is in fact justified.

Negatively, we have argued that where the Word was held to determine the human nature of Christ directly, operating as the single subject of all his actions, there was an incipient tendency to either some form of Apollinarianism or kenoticism. One way or the other the active humanity of Christ was neglected or undermined. As the discussion progressed it was apparent that the issue resolved itself into questions concerning the nature of Christ's humanity. Were the experiences of the man Christ Jesus continuous with our own? Did he stand before God as we do? Did being truly human mean not merely the possession of a catalogue of static human qualities, but also include acting and responding in a fully human way? If so it would suggest that the process by which Christ as man learnt of God was similar to our own religious experience, that is, it was mediated by the enlightening, encouraging, comforting, empowering and sanctifying work of the Holy Spirit.

The positive argument of this chapter has been that Christ's humanity was indeed of this sort. His role as the prototype of the Christian life and the nature of his priestly office whereby he gave up his life on behalf of his people and knew separation from God, both point to the reality of his active humanity in a manner which the tradition has often overlooked. We have also argued that Owen was in essence correct in holding that Christ revealed God, not immediately by his divine nature, but rather through his humanity as a man whom the Spirit has specifically anointed that he might bring good news to the poor. Finally, we suggested that it was possible to describe Jesus' self-consciousness as one which was integrated and continually developing, and therefore of the same nature as our own in its operation if not in its content. In short, we have argued from Owen that the experiences of the man Christ Jesus were continuous with our own.

The underlying assumption of the discussion has been that the integrity of Christ's human nature, understood in this active sense, can only be maintained if the divine Word is recognised as operating on it not directly or immediately, but rather indirectly through the Spirit. This assumption is based on the perception that our experience of the Spirit does not violate the integrity of our humanity. For although every spiritual act that we perform has its source in God's wisdom and will and flows from the redemptive life and work of Christ as that life is effectively imparted to us by the Spirit, nevertheless, our humanity is not bypassed or directly determined by the divine nature, rather our human mind, will and affections are enabled to function in a way which is wholly appropriate to their own being. Therefore, if Christ's human experiences were in fact much like our own, it would appear that his human attributes were not merely the passive instruments for divine thoughts, decisions or feelings, rather, they would have always operated actively in a fully human way knowing, serving, obeying and glorifying God as we do through the Holy Spirit.

But if this is indeed so, and Owen's argument that the divine Son acts on his own human nature only indirectly and by means of the Spirit is essentially correct, then it is right to conceive of the incarnate Christ in his humanity as living and responding to God in a manner which is in principle possible for us. In short, the way is open to conceive of him as the historical exemplification of the true nature of man. This would require that we estimate man not primarily in terms of an ideal past but rather in his relation to the person of Christ and his future in him. For we become fully human only as we are conformed to the one whom God put forward as the exemplar of true human existence.

In this context the person of Christ may not be considered merely as a transcendent reality functioning as some sort of cypher for the divine being and divorced from the history of Jesus. Our conformity is rather to Jesus Christ in the mundane experience of his historical existence, an existence marked by fears and trials, faith and hope, continually strengthened, comforted and inspired by the Spirit of God through suffering and temptation as he sought in loving obedience to accomplish the will of the Father. I would suggest that the practice, common in the earlier Christian tradition, of describing the goal of man as some form of divinisation is open to grave misinterpretation. Our destiny is not that we might be made divine but rather that we might at last become truly human.

The incarnation thus provides the strongest theological foundation for the assertion that human being is in itself intrinsically valuable. Sadly the Church's failure in the past to emphasise the full and active 'autokinetic' humanity of Jesus Christ contributed to her inability to develop this perspective. It was left to the humanists of the Renaissance to reassert the significance of man's life before death and the greatness of his human possibilities. Yet lacking christological foundation, 'belief' in man as such is bound to disappoint. It is only 'true' man, man as he has been made known in the life of the Rabbi from Nazareth, or man as he is brought into conformity to that life, who is able to bear the weight of such a creed.

3. Strange News from Another Star: An Anthropological Insight from Edward Irving

Graham McFarlane

Of the multiform problems involved in constructing a Christian anthropology there are two issues that merit specific attention. On the one hand, it has to take an account of and in some way explain the context of human sin as it ranges from the beguiling, through commonplace mediocrity to the diabolical.

On the other hand a meaningful Christian anthropology has to expound the exact status of Christ's humanity in light of this context. The point is heightened, in turn, if we accept as *a priori* the theological premiss that it is only in and through Jesus Christ that we have defined not only what is truly divine but also that which is truly human.

All this, in turn, has to be unfolded in light of immediate soteriological implications, within which, on the whole, the history of Christian hamartiology has understood 'sin', too often, to be, almost, an end in itself. Sin becomes a 'thing' for which account has to be given; a taint that is to be removed. Thus a barter soteriology is perpetuated in which focus all too often falls on that which is to be removed rather than the one who brings forgiveness and life. In this sense we talk of sin being construed as an end in itself.

But if focus is to be turned away from sin itself to the one who redeems, we confront immediate implications in the consequent christology that is constructed. Historically, it would appear that the lesser theological difficulty lay in giving priority to the familiar and all too observable and experienced, namely, the predictability of human sin, rather than on the kind of christology necessary to give meaning to the Christian proclamation of 'Good News' within the brokenness of created existence. Such christological activity involves addressing and grappling with traditional hamartiological and soteriological questions, which can be summarized thus:

1. What is it about human beings that makes it possible for them in their finitude to know the infinite God?

2. What is it about human beings that makes fallenness possible in such a radical way as to require the kind of redemption to which Christianity witnesses?[1]

The purpose of this paper is to present briefly the manner by which Edward Irving establishes a Christian anthropology which addresses both questions and the issues they involve, and in so doing shed light on his specific understanding of human being as that derived specifically from the incarnation of the second person of the Trinity as the human history of Jesus Christ.

Paradise Gained

According to Judeo-Christian cosmogonies, the arrival of human being onto the platform of history announces the highest form of created being. It is the culmination of the creator God's activity, after which is sabbath. For Irving, however, the creation of human being at this point is not to be considered as complete nor as an end in itself. Rather, it finds its ultimate meaning in the Creator's purpose for creation. This purpose Irving considers heterogenously. Firstly, from a *theological* perspective, the human creature exists in order that God may 'find the justification of his holiness, and the upholding of it forever'.[2] Human being exists in order that the invisible mind of God may be brought to light and God seen and known in his working over creation'.[3] Human being, therefore, is created with the express purpose of revealing 'unto all the creatures the invisible and infinite substance of the Godhead',[4] and to 'body forth God completely in all the features and powers of his invisible Godhead'.[5] Secondly, creation has a *christological* function: the great end of creation consists, for Irving, in revealing the Son of God in 'the creature form of the risen God-man,' thus enabling the creature 'to represent, to enact, and to enjoy a part of the Son's fulness (Col. i. 15-20)'.[6] Thirdly, there is an *anthropic* dimension: by virtue of the Creator's act of creation *ex nihilo*, the human being is being-in-dependence. It is so by virtue of the humble origins of human existence, for 'as (God) was to make it out of nothing, He would have it remember its nothingness in

---

1   D. H. Kelsey: 'Human Being', in i *Christian Theology*. Eds. P. Hodgson, R. King. London: SPCK, 1983, pp. - 167, p. 141.
2   CHF: 116.
3   op. cit.: 14.
4   MW. 7: 52.
5   CHF: 116.
6   MW. 7: 60, MW. 5: 386.

itself . . . to this single end of bringing the creature to apprehend the nothingness of its substance, and the absoluteness of its dependence upon the Divine will'.[7]

All these different but inter-related criteria, however, are subsumed under the ultimate purpose of God in creating human being, which Irving understands in the following manner:

> The purpose of God in creating man, was the manifestation and communication of His own glory unto the creatures which He had made, or which He was about to make; and to bring the creature wholly dependent upon Him, and to worship Him.[8]

Consequently, the apex of creation is found to rest not in human being itself but in its contingent dependence upon the One who brings finite being into existence and fulfills its ultimate history. For Irving, the creation of human being announces the arrival of a being-in-relation with the Creator, created with the express purpose of revealing the glory of God. But by what means does Irving present human being as that which proclaims the glory of God? This Irving does through his understanding of human being as *imago Dei*.

Irving's entire anthropology may be interpreted as an explication of his understanding of the tensive symbolism[9] contained in the term *imago Dei*. The original charter for human being he understands to consist in the command to be 'Godlike,' to be 'an image and likeness of God in the law and form of (its) being'.[10] Irving explicates the divine identity in terms of the Son as the image of the Father. This, in turn, becomes the exegetical principle by which he interprets human being as *imago Dei*. When the Creator proclaims and brings about the high end of creation, he does so not in generic terms of conformity to a bare essence, but as that which bears witness to his Son. The human creature is

---

[7] CW. 5: 239.

[8] Ibid.

[9] I am indebted to Sally E. Alsford's unpublished Ph.D. thesis, *Sin as a Problem of Twentieth Century Systematic Theology*, University of Durham, 1987, for insights into the meaning of symbol as a 'tensive symbol'. Alsford uses 'tensive symbol' solely in relation to Paul Ricoeur's doctrine of original sin, and defines it as 'an idea or doctrine which collects (and thus to some extent simplifies) and represents a range of meanings and issues,' (p. 282). I would wish to extend this and argue that the biblical notions of *imago Dei* and dominion serve the same purpose. It is as we rediscover the rich analogical wealth expressed in such symbols that the biblical presentation of human being may be rediscovered.

[10] PW. 2: 411.

created to be an image of God after the likeness of the Son. So Irving states,

> Within Himself from all eternity there was an image of Himself in the person of the Eternal Son: out of Himself that image is found in man; first in the person of Christ, and then in every one who is renewed after the image of God in righteousness and true holiness.[11]

From this we are able to address two aspects of his thought. Firstly, Irving maintains an inherent tension between an archaeological and a teleological interpretation of the *imago Dei*. Christ is both the $\dot{\alpha}\rho\chi\dot{\eta}$ and the $\tau\acute{\epsilon}\lambda o\varsigma$ of human being; that which is imaged and that which perfectly images. As such, in imaging the Son who is the express image of the Father, human being is seen to derive its being entirely from its relationship with God the Son. But what does it mean to talk of a christocentric interpretation of the *imago Dei* in terms of its $\dot{\alpha}\rho\chi\dot{\eta}$. For Irving it means that human being as *imago Dei* is derived from that which it mirrors. Here Irving can be seen as standing in a wholly Reformed interpretation of the *imago Dei*. He does so primarily in terms of reflection, and secondarily, as conformity. Human being reflects the image of the Son and does so by 'conformity of an intelligent will to the will and Word of God'.[12]

Irving's understanding of the Son as the image of the invisible Father essentially entails the notion of 'image' as reflection: the Son is the image and likeness of the invisible Father. This notion of imaging is inextricably linked to the idea of obedience on the part of the Son. However, Irving delineates this obedience in terms of the Son's dependence upon the Spirit. Thus, it is a reflection-in-dependence. If, in turn, we apply this notion of reflection to human being, we may extend to the human creature as *imago Dei* the same notion of reflection. As such, human being lacks an essential ability to perform its given created end, not merely by virtue of its finitude, but more importantly by virtue of its essential being as a finite reflection of the Son. As the Son depends on the Spirit in order to reveal the Father, so the human creature has been created to reflect this being-in-dependence and attains its full humanity only in dependence upon the Spirit. Thus, for Irving, although human being is created in the likeness of the Son, it performs this imaging by means of a specific relation

---

[11] op. cit.: 382.
[12] T. F. Torrance: *Calvin's Doctrine of Man*. London: Lutterworth Press, 1952, p. 80.

to the Spirit. The manner by which Irving delineates this pneumatic being-in-dependence will be addressed in more detail in the following sections. At this point it suffices to say that Irving echoes Torrance's comment on Calvin, that 'the *imago dei*, spiritually considered, has no momentum or security of its own, but depends entirely upon the grace of God and is maintained only in relation to that grace'.[13]

Throughout his writings, from the earliest sermons to the later apologetical writings, Irving is consistent in his insistence that human being is created as the image of God in order 'to act the divine part among earthly scenes'.[14] But how does Irving delineate the dynamics of such an enactment? 'Man,' he answers most concisely in the journal, *The Morning Watch*, 'was created for two ends: the first, "to be an image and likeness of God"; the second, "to have dominion over the creatures".' It is upon the former that we focus our attention, which is, he continues, 'descriptive of (man's) reasonable soul . . . fashioned on very purpose to be an image of God, who is Spirit; endowed with his affections of love and goodness, of truth and justice, of wisdom and understanding: . . . so that God without any accommodations should be able to speak his mind to man, and man without any conjecture should be able to understand it'.[15]

The image, therefore, does not consist merely of a moral propensity, nor even in the mutuality of human sexual differentiation.[16] Rather, Irving continues with his ontology of will by locating the capacity for image-bearing in the human will. It is this notion of the will that becomes the *leitmotiv* for Irving's doctrine of human being.

Intimately linked to the notion of human will as the means by which the divine and human meet, is the notion of freedom. Human being is the image of one who is unconstrained. Consequently, the image itself cannot be constrained.[17] It is because 'God is free and uncaused, being the cause of himself,' he states that 'man must have, and hath, such a part in his will, which within the creature-bound is caused by nothing, but is of itself the cause'.[18] Thus Irving maintains the notion of human being as image bearer of the creator of God in terms of the creature's will and its original freedom. The very constitution of human being

---

[13] Ibid.
[14] OG.: 78.
[15] MW. 5: 387.
[16] K. Barth: Church Dogmatics, III. i. 183f, 1958.
[17] PW. 2: 12.
[18] CHF: 116.

resides in the will, whereby the human creature 'is a figure of God; the will answering to the Father, in that it is a cause unto itself, not caused by things without or motives within, but free in its proper constitution to originate all thought and action'.[19]

This divine freedom from causality is revealed in God's ability both to be what he will himself to be and to remain so. This freedom from determinism, in turn, constitutes the ἀρχή of human existence. As God is perfectly free from any form of causation, so Irving argues, 'it is required that there should be in man, his image, a will which should be uncaused, the cause of itself; not overmastered by God, but left to act in its own liberty'.[20] Freedom of will in the human creature, therefore, reflects the very character of God, who is himself perfectly free and uncaused.

But why this element of uncausality? Firstly, as noted above, human being is constituted according to the Creator's design, whose desire it is that the human creature should be like him, and be so by its own volitional will, determined neither by the divine nor the human.[21] Secondly, and of more significance, is the derivation of the above from a purely christocentric ontology. As we have noted, human being is created in the image of the Son who, himself, is the image of the invisible Father. This the Son performs freely both in the economy of salvation and the inner trinitarian relations as the Son dependent upon the Spirit. As a consequence of being created image bearer of this God, the human creature is created to reflect God in its willingness to serve him freely, in a manner paralleling that of the Son.

Having delineated the form by which Irving explicates the unique position of the human creature, namely, an ontology of will, we are able now to outline the dynamics by which this *vinculum* is animated and personalised. Human being performs its destiny in and through its proper and willing response to the Creator's will. The latter in turn is an operation of the Divine purely in the realm of will. This is not merely a qualification of being, but one much more of grace, for, God 'would have the will of man to be recognised as the lord of all visible things'.[22] Thus, Irving outlines the Godward identity of the human creature by use of the tensive symbol, *imago Dei*, in order to present 'spiritual life' as 'the life of the spirit . . . the constant presence of a will to live so'.[23] In so doing, he presents not only human spirituality in

[19] MW. 7: 60.
[20] MW. 5: 388.
[21] Ibid.
[22] CHF: 14.
[23] op. cit.: 39.

terms of obedient will, but human 'perfection in terms of one whose will, word and work is in unison with God's.'[24]

Yet, whilst the human will is the meeting place between the Creator and the created, the Divine and the human, it is the purely material aspect of human existence that is, for Irving, the *conditio sine qua non* by which this occurs due to the fact that 'the body is the organ by which the spirit within a man manifests itself to the world'.[25]

It is this embodied reality that for Irving manifests how the creation of Adam surpasses the primary angelic order as the one fit to be the *imago Dei*, for incorporeal being before the creation of Adam had no need of a material body in order to perfect its being: it is pure spirit, perfect in its kind. But not so with Adam, who as the nexus between the spiritual and material introduces not only an altogether new form of created existence, but one that is superior to all others that precede it.

Thus the human creature is created, Irving argues 'first and noblest of all, to be (God's) own image and like-ness; but next, and only second to this, to be the heir, possessor, and lord of all (God's) created works, to have dominion, to rule for God, to possess and to enjoy the works of (God's) hands: this is an integrant part of man's creation; — to inherit the earth; . . . to have dominion over the beasts of the earth, the fish of the sea, and the fowls of the heaven,' and for Irving, 'this . . . is as much of man's essential being as it is to be holy as God is holy, and pure as He is pure'.[26]

It is by both loci that human being is immanent and transcendent: both 'being-in' and 'being-with'. As such, it is the *vinculum creationis*. Herein lies the original design of human being: 'a body of dust, and a spirit from God; by the one holding of the creature, by the other of the Creator; and so in (it)self forming a link between the creature and the Creator.'[27]

In summary conclusion to his analysis of 'Paradise Gained,' therefore, Irving is seen to present an anthropology determined by the use of the two symbols, *imago Dei* and the exercise of 'dominion'. Human being is being-with-God, *imago Dei*. This it performs both by imaging the Son, and doing so in dependence with the Spirit. But human being is also being-in-the-world, *imago mundi*, expressed in dominion and lordship. Both are pursued through an ontology of will. Through his obedient will the first Adam is image bearer. As embodied will, Adam is the

---

[24] CHF: 20.
[25] CW. 5: 454.
[26] PW. 2: 412.
[27] CHF: 20.

vinculum, the meeting point between the Divine and the created. Within this ontology of will Irving addresses the problem as to how human being in its finitude is able to know the infinite God: it does so as embodied will created after the image of the Son. Human being as *imago Dei*, therefore, is not primarily a statement about the creature, but an expression about its uniqueness within creation. It is to the centrality Irving gives to this object from which human being derives its unique status that we now turn.

Strange News from Another Star[28]

Epistemologically, the anthropological dimension to any given christology is of major importance. But from what direction do we approach our doctrine of human being within the context of *Heilsgeschichte*? Christian cosmogonies and cosmologies (theories about the origin of the universe, and treatises on the structure of creation), by and large, have explicated knowledge of the human in terms of the conflict between either an archaeological or a teleological interpretation of creation. On the whole, the dominant interpretation has been the former, the archaeological. The fall from an originally perfect state necessitates a return to the primordial state of perfection in which the first human beings were created. *Heilsgeschichte* is then interpreted in light of a return to this primordial state of perfection. Human being is interpreted in terms of its ἀρχή. Unfortunately, this facilitates a static and Aristotelian interpretation of human being: a qualitative commodity that, having lost its original identity, necessitates a restoration to the initial proto-type. But in light of our increasing knowledge of the human condition, such a 'proto-type' and any subsequent return to paradise lost comes, indeed, as 'strange news from another star'.

The teleological, on the other hand, may be understood as representing a more developmental and progressive interpretation of human history. Human being is interpreted in terms of its end. It incorporates an eschatological dimension which facilitates some sense of openness to the Creator God. Consequently, human being is liberated from the determinism of its past, to be conceived in dynamic and relational terms. It is from this direction Irving perceives the human story.

---

[28] Herman Hesse: *'Merkwürdige Nachricht von einem andern Stern.' Strange News from Another Star & Other Tales.* Trans. J. Wright. New York: Farrar, Strava & Groux, 1972.

I believe, he says, God hath ordained nature in its present form,
and established it according to its present laws, for the single
and express purpose of shadowing forth that future perfect
condition into which it is to be brought: so that from man down
to the lowest creation . . . everything containeth the presenti-
ment of its own future perfection.[29]

Irving's ontology of will emphasizes his western, Augustinian
heritage. Human being is distinguished from all other being
because it is *imago Dei*. As such, it belongs to the same order of
being as God. The ἀρχή of human being consists in partaking of
divine reality by virtue of intellect and reason.[30] Yet, his is not a
noetic anthropology: the human spirit is not identified strictly in
terms of the rational. Nor is it guilty of the self-analysis and
introspection inherent in Augustine's integration of trinitarian
theology with human psychology. The human self is not an end in
itself. Rather, it finds its meaning in relation to an Other.
Consequently, for Irving, the human will designates a
hermeneutical rather than purely anthropological concept: it
finds its meaning in the *imago Dei* which is itself derivative of that
which it images.

This element in Irving's thought is not, however, the only aspect
in which he transcends his western heritage. Within his theological
interpretation of human being Irving attempts to overcome the
inherent hamartiological difficulties of a purely archaeological
interpretation of human being. This he does by neither rejecting
one for, nor pitting one against the other. Rather, he balances the
two by means of a dialectic which focuses on what each specifies
about the order of creation. Firstly, he maintains the belief that
God creates all things perfect. Within this essentially archaeo-

---

[29] CW. 1: 73-74.
[30] See *Sermon on Education* 8. Here Irving outlines the three original
capacities of the soul, held by all human beings to greater or lesser
degrees. Firstly, there is *scientific* knowledge and understanding
whereby we know and understand the natural world by means of our
five senses as explored and examined by our understanding. Secondly,
there is *personal* knowledge: the capacity of self-understanding,
conscience, moral judgment, psychology, social relations of family and
government, all of which Irving identifies as 'all that inward activity
of spirit, and outward condition of life, which distinguishes man from
the lower creatures,' (p. 8). Thirdly, there is *spiritual* knowledge, 'the
power of knowing, and worshipping, and obeying the true God'. Only
a form of education which gives place and dignity to each of these
respective areas of human activity and knowledge is 'liberal, catholic,
and complete,' (ibid.).

logical and primordial state of perfection, there is assimilated the twofold destiny of human being in its intrinsic relatedness with the Creator. Thus Irving argues that,

> It is of the nature of God to create all things perfect and blessed in their kind; and we certainly know that man was so created, and the dominion over which he ruled. There was no breach of peace amongst all the creatures over whom he held the mastery, nor between his wife and him, nor between God and his living soul, nor among the elements of creation, nor anywhere within all the bounds of his habitation.[31]

However creation is also a teleological act. Its *being* is derived from its intended *becoming*. The sole purpose for all that is created is that it may express a future perfection under the sovereignty of God. Human being is perfect both in its ἀρχή and its τέλος. But each state of perfection has meaning, however, only in its subsumation within the Christ-event. It is both as *imago Dei* and *imago mundi* that we may understand this dialectical use of perfection. On the one hand Adam is the perfect being as first of his human kind, as the ἀρχή of human being within the locus of creation. Alternatively, Adam is the one who is becoming perfect as one who stands in relation to the τέλος of human being, which, for Irving, is Christ. Therefore, the τέλος of human being is subsumed within the *locus of Christ*. Irving's christology dictates his doctrine of human being. Human being is in its becoming as a type of the incarnate Son, the Christ: through him and for him are all things created, from him does humanity derive its identity, of *him* it is the image. Its creation, fall and subsequent redemption are located in the person of the incarnate Son. The full expression of human being, therefore, is not that which is presented in Adam, in creation. Rather, it is that which is revealed in the proto-type, Christ, in the history of redemption.

Here Irving stands in harmony with neglected elements in his own tradition. He expands elements that can be found in the earlier anthropologies of Irenaeus and Luther. Firstly, he parallels Irenaeus's insistence that human being is created, that it receives growth, is strengthened, abounds, falls, but recovers, is glorified, and ultimately sees God.[32] Both Irving and Irenaeus insist that to taste of sin is to bring about a greater state of human being. The experience of knowing then shunning evil, produces true human character.[33]

---

[31] CW. 5: 322.
[32] Irenaeus *Against Heresies*. IV. xxviii. 3. Ante-Nicene Christian Library, vol. V, Edinburgh: T. & T. Clark, 1880.
[33] op. cit. III. xx. 2; IV. xxxix. 2: V. iii. 1.

Secondly, Irving echoes the sentiments found in Luther's exegesis of the Genesis story. For Luther, even if had Adam not sinned, 'he would still have lived a physical life in need of food, drink, rest. He would have grown, procreated, etc., until *he would have been translated by God to the spiritual life* in which he would have lived without any animal qualities'.[34] It is this element of translation from one state to another that is paralleled in both writers. But Irving makes more thorough use of a christological distinction than Luther in order to distinguish between the first and second Adams. At this point we are able to comment fully on Irving's doctrine of human being as *imago Dei*. Within his ontology of will he asserts that human and divine existences are of the same order of being: creation is perfected in redemption. Yet, this is not to suggest that human being is of the same essential being as God. Rather, it expresses the *quality* of analogy. The boundary of this analogy is clearly set within a trinitarian setting: although 'man was created in the image of God, he was not so in the same sense in which Christ is called "the brightness of the Father's glory, and the express image of His person".' This differentiation is then given full expression in Irving's exegesis of Paul's distinction between the two Adams in 1 Corinthians 15. Irving's interpretation of the 'natural man' differs from Luther's in that whilst Luther denotes the Adamic language generically, Irving does so specifically.[35] Thus he states:

> In this passage we are taught that Adam was not a spiritual creature in the sense in which we are spiritual, who are born again of the Spirit by the quickening power of the Lord Jesus Christ: nor was he a creature in the dignity into which we are adopted by faith . . . Whatever distinction there is between a soul and spirit — and such a distinction is continually preserved in Scripture — that same distinction there is between the generation of Adam and the regeneration of Christ.[36]

[34] Luther: *Commentary on Genesis*, XLII, 65, 66, p. 86. Saint Louis: Concordia Publishing House, 1958.

[35] The translation from which Irving works is as follows: 'It is sown a natural body (or a body proper to a soul), it is raised a spiritual body (or a body proper to a spirit); there is a natural (soulish) body, and there is a spiritual body. And so it is written, The first man Adam was made a living soul, the second Adam a life-giving Spirit. Howbeit, that was not first which is spiritual, but that which is of the soul; and afterward that which is spiritual. The first man is of the earth, earthy; the second man is the Lord from Heaven. As is the earthy, such are they also that are earthy; and as is the heavenly, such are they also that are heavenly. And as we have borne the image of the earthy, so we shall also bear the image of the heavenly.'

[36] CW. 5: 81.

What is of importance to note is that Irving derives his understanding about the ἀρχή of human being ultimately from Christ. The first Adam he identifies in terms of '*soul*'. Herein lies the primary criterion for Irving's developmental anthropology. 'In that form of being called *the soul*, after which Adam was created,' Irving argues there is 'a natural incapacity for receiving or knowing the things (of) the Spirit ... that this is a form of being preparatory for a higher and more perfect one, which God might have perhaps given to (the) first parents if they had stood faithful unto Him who created them. They were perfect in that kind in which they were created ... but that kind was not of the perfectest, which yet awaited them, and to which they perhaps would have been translated if they had not fallen.'[37] In this form of existence Adam had little knowledge of God beyond that of Creator. Herein lies the interpretation of human being within a thoroughly trinitarian hermeneutic. In the light of both the revelation of the trinitarian God in and through Christ, and this developmental interpretation of human being, Irving asserts that:

> Of God's spiritual being I am in great doubt whether (Adam) could have any distinct apprehension or knowledge; because Paul expressly saith, that the natural man, or the man of the soul, of which Adam was the perfect form, knoweth not the things of the Spirit of God: he could not know the Father, who is known only by the Son, who was not yet come forth from the bosom of the Father; and not knowing the Son he could not know the Spirit whose procession succeedeth that of the Son. More than the knowledge of a Creator he could not have. His being was only, if I may so speak, preparatory to a spiritual being.[38]

In this manner human being is presented as a dynamic and developing link between all forms of existence, from that of the purely immanent and created world, through the transcendent created realm of finite spirit, to that of transcendent trinitarian Being: Father, Son and Spirit. Human being is the *vinculum* between all these forms of existence, not essentially, but derivatively. It is so, firstly, as embodied will, as a form of being greater than that which precedes it, whether corporeal or non-corporeal. It is because the human creature makes visible the invisible functions of pure spirit in its understanding, righteousness and love within space and the possession of matter, that Irving understands the creation of pure spirit (angelic life) to be a type

[37] Ibid.
[38] op. cit. 82.

of the embodied spirit, human being. Secondly, human being
becomes the *vinculum* solely in its relation to Christ, the image of
the Father, the true *imago Dei*. Lest we think anthropocentrically,
Irving describes human being as but a type itself of 'that Divine
form of being which Christ was to be'.[39] Consequently, the first
Adam is a *type* of the second.[40]

Herein lies the dual dignity Irving ascribes to human being: it
has, speaking metaphorically, both a horizontal and vertical
dimension. Horizontally, it is the fullest creative expression by
God: all things point to the arrival of human being onto the
platform of history. They are but a type of the one who is image
bearer. In *this* being meet the hitherto unrelated dimensions of
spirit and matter. But to stop at this 'high' and optimistic picture
of man is not merely to misrepresent reality as it now stands, but
to belittle the true source and measure of human dignity. This
Irving posits within the vertical realm: it is in and through the
relation of human being to the incarnate Son that he identifies the
true worth of human being. But before we can appreciate fully
what Irving means by this we must now turn our attention to the
context within which human being now finds itself, and into
which the Son was incarnated.

Paradise Lost
Contemporary human identity has become a cauldron of conflicting and relativised ego-expressions jostling for a safe anchor
amidst the chaos of pluriformity. As it reaches out to extend the
perimeters of its knowledge and dominion, it appears to become,
at the same time, more fragmented and alienated from the
richness and creative profusion promised in the Eden mandate to
have dominion and to prosper. It is into this context that Irving
speaks, a context embraced within the Genesis story of Eden and
exile, of garden and wilderness. The Genesis presentation of
creation with its order of relatedness wherein Adam is placed lord
and from which he subsequently falls, with catastrophic results,
is no Münchhausen. It expresses that which adumbrates most
eloquently the human story.

As a result of the Fall, human being is no longer the embodied
spirit which exists creatively between two 'limiti', as *imago Dei*
and *imago mundi*, as one created and called to exist in that
creative tension between the opposites of immanence and tran-

---

[39] op. cit. 93.
[40] See *Ben Ezra*, ccxxxff for a detailed outline of Irving's presentation of
Christ as Prophet, Priest and King. Also, CW. 5: 81.

scendence. It no longer knows the dynamic freedom of existing within its unbounded contest of possibilities. Rather, it is exiled to a wilderness, losing the sense of the apophatic, of the possible. It becomes grounded in the predictable and the mediocre — in its own fallenness and predilection to sinning against its Creator, self and environs. As a result, the intended profusion and creativity for humanity by its Creator is exchanged for a 'desert place': the structure of relatedness with God, self and creation is exchanged for a lie. Through time and cultural persuasion the human lot is accepted as an expression of the *status quo*. Ultimately, the dislocation of human being brought about by the Fall presumes 'false shadows for true substances'.[41] In this context, Irving's stress upon the immediacy of the Genesis story is a call to remembrance, for, he advocates, 'the truth is that men have forgotten what the fall was; and how really it is now to be perceived in every thing, without exception, pertaining to the age that is now'.[42]

As we have noted, Irving's teleological anthropology presents Adam as perfect, yet incomplete. Human being cannot have been created in its full perfection, he attests, in light both of its subsequent demise and the appearance of Christ. For he argues, 'if the creation had been perfect and sufficient while yet the Christ was unconstituted, then why should there be a Christ at all? There cannot be two perfections, there cannot be two unchangeables, otherwise there were two gods'.[43] Thus, Adam is merely the type of Christ: creation in the unfallen state existing only to make way for creation in its fallen state, for if Adam is the apex of creation, there can be no divine remedy for a fall and redemption seen to be a mere after thought with no guarantee offered in the redeemed state against a further fall. Consequently, for Irving, creation is preparatory for, and perfected in, redemption.

Eden, therefore, is created in order to show the incompleteness of human being. It is preparatory for an even higher state of finite existence. Here, Irving stands apart from the traditional Augustinian emphasis upon a 'static' cosmology. Rather, Adam's self-situatedness manifests that 'the creation, all good though it was, is not the accomplishment but only the beginning of God's

---

[41] W. Shakespeare, *Titus Andronicus*, Act 3, scene 2.
[42] CW. 5: 43.
[43] CW. 5: 98.
[44] MW. 7: 63.

purpose'.[44] The τέλος of human being is delineated in light of the divine command to refrain from eating the fruit of the tree of the knowledge of good and evil. What Irving appears to be implying is that although Adam is created with the capacity to know such knowledge, it is not necessarily to be by virtue of willful disobedience. Irving goes on to argue for two consequences of such an epistemic state. Firstly, the teleological: it is a state higher than that of Adam's original createdness. Why? Because it is a knowledge not merely of good, but of good *and evil*. Secondly, the ontological: it is a state possessed of the Godhead itself. As such, it can hardly be an evil state. Thus, it must be a state capable of being attained by other means than that pursued by the first couple.[45] Consequently, Irving perceives the τέλος of human being to be not only epistemic but existential: the ability not only to distinguish between good and evil, but to choose the good, to *be imago Dei*.

Irving is able now to move into the second stage of human-being-in-its-becoming. He moves his anthropology from the primary created state, that of simple goodness communicated directly by the hand of God, to the second, the Fall, the state of the knowledge of good and evil, fallen into *by disobedience*. He argues that

> It was necessary that Adam should pass into a fallen state, to shadow forth Christ in the fallen state, and to this very end was paradise created with all its ordinances.[46]

Irving approaches the fall of human being from two different but complementary perspectives: the cosmological and the ontological. The former, and purely negative, perceives the fall as permitted in order to distinguish the Creator from the creature, as well as affirm the order of relatedness that exists between humanity and its Creator. Thus Irving states that,

> In order . . . to preserve distinctness between the invisible and absolute God and the visible limited creature, it was necessary that the creature should fall: and, by falling, should know the end and inferiority that is in itself; and that the goodness which it had originally, is a goodness derived from another source than itself, seeing there hath not been, in itself, the power of

---

[45]   Although Irving is never explicit about this in his writings, it is a logical implication from his teleological anthropology.
[46]   MW. 7: 63.
[47]   CW. 5: 419. Also, CW. 5: 239.

retaining it.[47]

Why does he argue thus? Irving understands the necessity of positing a clear distinction between the Creator and that which he creates. Thus, human being is wholly separate from its Creator, with little or no knowledge of spiritual life or Fatherly love. In its primal state, the creation does not reflect its intended $\tau\acute{\epsilon}\lambda o\varsigma$. Rather, as interpreted through Irving's thoroughly christocentric hermeneutic,

> a creation out of God was not the ultimate end of the purpose,
> but a creation united to God, and yet not mixed with him,
> through the union of a creature redeemed with the manhood
> taken into the person of the Son.[48]

We return again to his central concern: creation and human being have meaning solely in and through the incarnate Son, for it is only in *him* that the divine and created meet in fullest expression. Despite its archaeological perfection, the perfection of creation rests not in the greatest expression of divine *fiat*, human being, but in the incarnation of the Son. The issuing forth of the Son in incarnation by the Father through the Spirit, Irving asserts, is intimately associated with the development of human being in its becoming that which the Creator intends. But it is a 'becoming' not by a return to primal perfection. This is no recreation: such would infer regressive and static historical consequences, for such an interpretation of the human story would make dubious the Creator's ability to maintain his creation. Rather, it is the perfecting of creation through redemption.

But in what way and by what means does the Creator bring about this $\tau\acute{\epsilon}\lambda o\varsigma$? To answer this we must explore the *hamartiological* dynamics within Irving's cosmology. These he links to the divine permission of a fall from grace.

Irving's hamartiology is delineated from the viewpoint of human being in its becoming that which the Creator intends. The fall of Adam does not take God by surprise. Neither does it hinder that which God intends for his creation. Rather, it is an act of human disobedience both known and foreseen, and permitted by God.[49] It is this aspect of foreknowledge that Irving will link intimately with this doctrine of Christ, as we shall see towards the end of our paper. The introduction of human *disobedience* into the scene of

[48]   MW. 7: 63.
[49]   CW. 5: 10.
[50]   op. cit.: 103.

history is necessary to the Creator's plan.[50] It is this somewhat nervous theodicean tension between the necessity of sin, on the one hand, with the preclusion of divine culpability on the other, that Irving grasps and makes explicit to his doctrine of human being in its becoming. This necessity, far from embarrassing the Godhead, is the means by which the full grace and love of God will be revealed.

But Irving is adamant that sin is not the creation of God: rather, it comes about by the uncaused will of the creature.[51] It is that for which only an initially free will may be held responsible. It is 'a condition of the creature' and one that reveals how inferior the creature is to the Creator.[52] Adam's 'lie' does not create any 'thing' or 'creature'. The lie of human being has expression only by the light of the true being, the incarnate Son in whose image human being is created. It has no life of its own, but is rather the parasitic resistance of a free creature against God. It is not a thing in itself, but 'the evil condition of a thing'. It is 'a condition of the creation, proceeding from the freedom of the will of man, who was invested with creation's weal or creation's woe'.[53] It is a state of being: 'it is the *state* of a creature — the *second* state of a creature,'[54] the state of sin.

The horror of the first act that brings about this new state is manifested in its deadly consequences. It is an 'eternal and unchangeable... condition' into which the human will is brought. It is an alienation of the will from its proper disposition: 'it is a spiritual act against a Spirit, against the good and gracious Father of spirits'.[55] This emphasis on the will as the seat of sin, and the identification of will with spirit, supports Irving's insistence upon the irremediable consequences of the fall. When he addresses the angelic fall, a fall from a purely spiritual state of existence, he insists there can be no reconstruction of the former state of relations with the Divine: for there is no higher created state than the spiritual. Indeed, as Coleridge states, 'if it be hard to explain how Adam fell; how much more hard to solve how purely spiritual beings could fall?'[56] But such an irremediable state is not the destiny of embodied spirit. What hope is there, asks Irving, for 'the

---

[51] CW. 5: 10.
[52] op. cit.: 99, 239.
[53] PW. 2: 405.
[54] CW. 5: 218.
[55] op. cit.: 18.
[56] S. T. Coleridge, *Literary Remains*, vol. 3, London: William Pickering, 1883, p. 330.

will of a spirit which of its own accord hath swerved away, which did not choose to stand when all was in its favour?'[57] There is none, he insists. A revelation of divine omnipotence is, of itself, unable to bridge the chasm created by Adam's action. Irving's entire thrust is to show how the human predicament may be resolved only by 'the revelation of more persons than one in the Godhead'.[58] It comes as no surprise, therefore, that he interprets the Son's work as that of redeeming the human will from its self-inflicted bondage.

But in response to whether God's purposes could have been achieved without a fall, Irving is hesitant to state, except to say that 'this was the best way of accomplishing it'.[59] Thus he states that, 'while I assert the necessity of sin as a part of the great scheme, I wholly disallow that any creature was made for sin, but every creature for Christ'.[60] The salient point here is that Irving approaches the problem of sin and its eruption into previously perfect environs not in the light of sin but of Christ, for 'the end of creation was the Christ'. Despite this, Irving treads a very narrow line of argument, implying an inherent necessity to sin, for he goes on to say, 'this is the great end and purpose of sin in the creation of God, which, if you consider it well, is as essential to the fulness of the scheme, as is creation itself'.[61]

Yet how can sin be necessary, whilst God have no responsibility for it? This is a question Irving does not address directly. However, he appears to jeopardise his theodicy by the manner in which he stresses the necessity of sin. This I believe to be a fair criticism of Irving unless one considers the two different but complementary perspectives by which he approaches the fall. Theologically, he defends the Godhead from any culpability on the grounds that the primal freedom of uncaused human will, and the exalted position of human being as *vinculum* between the immanent and the Transcendent, safeguard his theodicy. Teleologically, although God cannot be responsible for the fall, he permits it in order to fulfill his plan for creation. The appearance of the incarnate Son into the arena of human history as the τέλος of human being affirms that the fall is permitted in order to bring about this τέλος. However, if this latter, christocentric element to his theodicy is addressed outwith its relation to the former anthropological

[57] CW. 5: 18.
[58] Ibid.
[59] CW. 5: 203.
[60] op. cit. 103.
[61] op. cit. 98.

responsibility, Irving is not only misrepresented, but interpreted as making sin an end in itself. This is not the case, although it is a criticism, the implications of which he fails to overcome in any fully satisfactory manner. However, from his very earliest writings and on he states the context within which any hamartiological discussion should occur:

> The Fall is not an origin — creation is before it: and the purpose of God in Christ is before creation, and is the true origin of all being, the true end of all revelation.[62]

We shall comment on the significance of this chronology for Irving once we have commented on the more positive aspect of Irving's discussion on the fall of human being: the ontological. Irving understands the fall to have been permitted firstly, in order to bring about a higher form of existence. As we have noted above, it brings the creature into a knowledge of good and evil. But it also initiates the human creature to be the bearer of God's wrath against sin. Although the *imago Dei* is deformed and the body destined to death, human being remains accountable for its capacity as image bearer, for human being is not immediately consumed as a result of the fall. If this were so, human being would be a 'monument of wrath consumed' rather than a 'free-will actor of God's wrath'.[63] It is the God-given capacity to overcome sin and in so doing declare God's sentence upon it that affirms the dignity of human being even in its fallen state.[64]

Secondly, Irving understands the fall of Adam as preparatory to the arrival of the 'God-man' onto the scene of human history.[65] Herein is his thoroughly christocentric interpretation of the human story. If there were no fall, there could be no knowledge available to the creature of the eternal Son, neither in his offices as prophet, priest and king, nor in his names as Jesus, Christ and Lord. Consequently, within Irving's ontology, 'the fall is as essential for giving the God-man His dignity over and above the creatures, as it is for teaching the creature its distinctness from

---

[62] LD: 499.
[63] PW. 2: 153.
[64] This for Irving is only a possibility because there is an order of being prior to that of creation, namely, sacrifice. It is because creation has its being and meaning in and through the Lamb slain before the creation of the world that not only is sin already accounted for in its relation to a holy creator, but that the character of God is vindicated before any violation or offence occurs.
[65] CW. 5: 91.
[66] op. cit.: 423.

the invisible and incomprehensible Godhead'.[66]

Firstly, as we have noted, the soulish, earthy existence of the first Adam, is preparatory for the spiritual and more perfect second Adam.[67] But, secondly we have noted that this anthropological maxim has significance only in light of the anterior, christological assertion that such an event of falling has already been accounted for. At the very heart of Irving's thinking is the concern to give account for why God could create a human being which, although perfect in its kind as the first of creation, could rebel against its Creator in such a way that this act be understood as part of its development. Herein, I believe, lies the significance of the christological priority Irving brings to his doctrine of human being. The human creature is not only that which is created in the image of the Son, nor is it that whose being is in its becoming. What underlies all that Irving presents in both loci is the primacy he gives to the self-giving of the Son in obedience to the Father before any act of creation itself. Anterior both to the creation of human being and to its subsequent fall is that which Irving perceives to be of greatest import.

This he understands in terms of an ontology of *sacrifice*, which is the force behind his entire argument. He has argued that creation is not an end in itself. We have noted that its meaning is derived from the Creator's purposes. Yet Irving is not content to focus solely upon God's gracious action in atonement for sin. This is only of secondary importance. Rather, that which is of primary importance is how one may defend against committed sin.[68] This defence Irving finds in the ontological significance of Christ as 'the Lamb slain before the foundation of the world'. As such, sacrifice is of a prior ontological order to creation, whose full significance is not found in an event contained within space-time boundaries. Rather, it is a consideration 'proper to God Himself . . . (who) is in the essence of His being the Holy One, who cannot be controverted or contradicted, and hath no indulgence of sin whatever'. Consequently, the Creator himself takes account of any subsequent indulgence of sin. Thus Irving argues:

> Abhorrence of sin, and destruction to it, is the way of death, is an indefeasible constitution of the Godhead, ratified and made sure before creation, in order to be creation's beacon against sin.[69]

[67] CW. 5: 80-86.
[68] PW. 2: 165.
[69] Ibid.

Although human sin had real consequences and perverts the historical inheritance of all descendants of Adam, the Creator is not impotent, nor are his intentions thwarted. Of much greater import is the fact that when sin arose in the breast and mind of creation's lord, although a serious act against the constitution of God himself, it was, nevertheless, an act against that which God himself had 'already realized and declared' within himself by virtue of the Son's obedience to be the slain lamb.[70]

Consequently, Irving is able to defend an interpretation of the incarnation that takes seriously not only the human condition of sin, but also one that gives content to the dynamics of the incarnation with regards the humanity assumed by the Son. In this sense, Irving establishes a foundation upon which he may answer the questions asked at the beginning of this paper. He has established a teleological hermeneutical key for interpreting human being, given a basis for asserting the uniqueness of human being, and assessed the significance of sin and its erruption into human history. However, most importantly, his highly christocentric ontology enables him to take up and grapple with the very 'stuff' of the incarnation; the very humanity of Christ.

For Irving the humanity assumed by the incarnated Son is of pivotal importance on two theological fronts. Firstly, the soteriological: God can deal with sin, yet in a manner that avoids falling into impersonal barter-soteriology. Secondly, the anthropological: the eruption of sin into creation can be accounted for by the very development of human being both in being created through and as an image of the Lamb slain before the foundation of the world, and in being perfected, not as a re-creation of the first Adam, but as the fulfillment of a completely new humanity that lives in relation to the Father through the Spirit given only on account of the work of the Son.

In so doing, Irving provides the framework within which the dynamics of the incarnation may be expounded in such a manner that gives meaning to a relatively undeveloped element of his tradition most succinctly posited by Tertullian:

> Why talk of a heavenly flesh, he says, when you have no grounds to offer us for your celestial theory? Why deny it to be earthy, when you have the best reasons for knowing it to be earthy? He hungered under the devil's *temptation*; He thirsted with the woman of Samaria; He wept over Lazarus; He trem-

---

[70] op. cit.: 164-165.

bles at death (for 'the flesh', as He says, 'is weak'); At last He
pours out blood. These, I suppose, are celestial marks?[71]

What is it about human being that makes fallenness possible in
such a radical way as to require the kind of redemption to which
Christianity witnesses? It is, for Irving, that which resides ultimately within an ontology of will: of a Son willing to be the
sacrifice preceding any act of creation, and of a creature who, in
dependence upon the Spirit to perform the Father's will, not only
willingly redeems a creation from the wrath of a holy Creator, but
who, in doing so, raises creation's lord to a new and unbounded
context of possibilities.

---

[71] Tertullian: *On the Flesh of Christ*. The Ante-Nicene Fathers, vol. III,
Buffalo: The Christian Literature Publishing Co., 1885, p. 530.

Abbreviations

CHF   *Christ's Holiness in Flesh, the Form, Fountain Head, and
Assurance to Use of Holiness in Flesh*. Edinburgh: John
Lindsay & Co., 1831.

CS   *The Doctrine Held by the Church of Scotland Concerning the
Human Nature of Our Lord, As Stated in Her Standards*.
Edinburgh: John Lindsay & Co., 1830.

CW   *The Collected Writings of Edward Irving in Five Volumes*. Ed.
Rev. G. Carlyle, London: Alexander Strahan & Co., 1864.

LD   *The Last Days: A Discourse on the Evil Character of These our
Times: Proving them to be the 'Perilous Times' of the 'Last
Days'*. London: R. B. Sulley and W. Burnside, 1828.

MW   *The Morning Watch*. Vols. V, VII, London: James Fraser,
1833.

OCD   *The Orthodox and Catholic Doctrine of our Lord's Human
Nature. Set forth in four parts*. London: Baldwin and Craddock,
1830.

OCLHN   *The Opinions Circulating Concerning our Lord's Human
Nature, Tried By The Westminster Confession of Faith*. Edinburgh: John Lindsay & Co., 1830.

OG   *For the Oracles of God, Four Orations. For Judgment to Come,
An Argument, in 9 Parts*. London: T. Hamilton, 1823.

PW   *The Prophetical Works of Edward Irving In Two Volumes*.
London: Alexander Strahan, 1867.

4. Persons in Relation: John Macmurray

John Aves

The basis of this paper will be the concept of the person as given in Macmurray's Gifford lectures delivered in 1953-54, entitled *The Self as Agent* and *Persons in Relation*. These lectures are the fruition of Macmurray's philosophical career at Manchester, Johannesburg, Oxford, London and Edinburgh Universities. Because of the novel nature of Macmurray's view it will be necessary to give a lengthy introduction to how he arrived at his concept and to quote extensively from his work before making my comments.

Why be concerned with the person

Macmurray believed that the task of philosophy was to make sense of human experience — religious, moral, aesthetic, social and scientific. In the opening chapters of *The Self as Agent* he makes clear his belief that, (we are) far from making any unified sense of human experience, we are in the middle of the 'crisis of the personal'. He explains this by referring to two aspects of the social situation.

> One of these is the tendency towards an apotheosis of the state; the other the decline in religion. The two are intimately connected; since both express a growing tendency to look for salvation to political rather than religious authority . . . . The apotheosis of political authority involves the subordination of the personal aspect of life to its functional aspect.[1]

Writing on religion and its decline (which is worth quoting in full because of its contemporary relevance):

> Such a decline betrays and in turn intensifies a growing insensitiveness to the personal aspects of life and a growing indifference to personal values. Christianity in particular is the exponent and guardian of the personal and the function of organised Christianity in our history has been to foster and maintain the personal life and to bear continuous witness in

[1] John Macmurray, *The Self as Agent*, London, 1957, p.29.

symbol and doctrine to the ultimacy of personal values. If this influence is removed or ceases to be effective, the awareness of personal issues will tend to be lost in the pressure of functional preoccupations, by all except those who are by nature specially sensitive to them. The sense of personal dignity as well as personal unworthiness will atrophy, with the decline in habits of self-examination. Ideals of sanctity or holiness will begin to seem incomprehensible or even comical. Success will tend to become the criterion of rightness, and that will spread through society a temper which is extroverted, pragmatic and merely objective, for which all problems are soluble by better organisation. In such conditions the religious impulses of men will attach themselves to persons who wield political power and will invest them with a personal authority over the life of the community and its members. The state is then compelled to perform the functions of a church (for which by nature it is radically unfitted).[2]

The Failure of Philosophy

The crisis of the personal is also shown in the failure of philosophy to deal with the whole of human experience. In broad and sweeping terms Macmurray criticises the period from Descartes toHume for conceiving reality in terms of the mathematical form which proved adequate for the determination of the material world but not for the self and its activity as a thinker. The second phase which covers the period from Hegel to Whitehead conceived reality in terms of the organic form but failed to find a place again for the individual. Present day developments with Existentialism or Logical Empiricism are no more adequate. Empiricism concentrates on the narrow meaning of language, whereas the Existentialist forsakes the rigours of philosophical method.

The fundamental error of critical philosophy according to Macmurray is the primacy it gives to the self as an isolated thinker or ego. He shows this by a more detailed criticism of Kant and Descartes. Kant had made a distinction between the world of appearances and the world of things in themselves. He had done so to find a place for morality and science faced with the challenge of the Romantic philosophy of Hamann which reduced all knowledge to a form of aesthetic intuition. For Kant the world of appearances was the determinate world, the categories for the understanding of it were provided by the mind. Hence one could never know the world behind the appearances in itself. For the sake of morality it was necessary to posit the existence of human freedom, immortality and God. How though are the two worlds

[2] *Ibid.* pp. 30-31

related? Macmurray believes that here Kant failed to give a unified account of human experience; he gives as an example the experience of moral struggle between the instincts (part of the determinate world) and duty (part of the world of freedom). How can a person be fully a part of both? Secondly, Macmurray attempts to show that though Kant began with the primacy of theoretical reasoning, he ended by showing that it could only give rules for practical action.

> To the question, "How can I know that what I do is right?" Kant's answer strictly expressed is that I cannot, since the objective of moral action is indeterminable. At most I can know how to act rightly. By implication, something similar must be said in the theoretical field. To the question, "How can I know what I should think?" the proper critical answer must be, "You cannot; what you know is how to think rightly in conformity with the rules which reason lays down for the employment of understanding".[3]

Thirdly, Macmurray points to the inadequacy of Kant's understanding of religion as a prop to the weakness of human nature, and his insistence that the ground of religion is morality. This criticism spills over into Kant's inability to account for personal relations. For if we begin with the primacy of the 'I think' then there can be no 'you' or 'thou' addressing one but simply another 'I' with nothing to differentiate them. 'For thought is inherently private, and any philosophy which takes its stand on the primacy of thought, which defines the Self as a Thinker, is committed formally to an extreme logical individualism'.[4] In further demonstrating the inadequacy of critical philosophy, Macmurray naturally engages also with Descartes, particularly his method of radical doubt. He asks:-

> Is it not *prima facie* unlikely that the effort to extend doubt systematically to the limits of possibility should issue in an extension of certainty? Is it not more likely that our capacity for scepticism is as unlimited as our credulity and increases, like all our powers with exercise?... The method of doubt rests upon an assumption which should be made explicit, that a reason is required for believing but none for doubting'.[5]

Descartes' method means the disruption of the integrity of the self through a dualism of practical and theoretical activity.

---

[3] *Ibid*. p. 67.
[4] *Ibid*. p. 71
[5] *Ibid*. p. 76.

We are asked to embark upon a purely theoretical activity which isolates itself from the influence of all practical elements since these must introduce bias and prejudice, in the hope of attaining a knowledge which will take precedence over beliefs by which in practice we live.[6]

Change of Standpoint

In the light of these inadequacies, Macmurray proposes a complete change of standpoint from the primacy of the *cogito*, to the primacy of the self as agent and constituted by his relationship with another person. This is an entirely different way of envisaging the person, rooted as we are in equating the person with the individual self.[7] To conceive the Person as primarily an agent as constituted by personal relations involves Macmurray in a transformation of many traditional assumptions. For example, in the field of perception, whereas the cogito position was closely bound up with a visual model which tended to encourage a dualism of subject and object, he argues instead for the primacy of the tactual, given as we experience the resistance or the support of the other which can be material, organic or personal. Robustly he tells us that the problem of human freedom does not arise because all knowledge is of the past as we have attained it in action, and is determined because it belongs to the past. It is nonsense to deny human freedom, because in the light of the 'I do' it is always related to the future.

> To act is to determine the future: the past is already determinate. Knowledge, then, in its primary form, is the theoretical determination of the past in action. The freedom of the agent then, so far from being incompatible with the possibility of knowledge is the ground of that possibility.[8]

Theoretical Activity

What place has theoretical activity in Macmurray's concept? In several places in the lectures, he talks of the logical form of the personal, as being constituted by a negative. Applied to thought, this means that the positive aspect of the person is activity; but for

---

[6] *Ibid.* p. 78.
[7] See Nicholas Lash, *Easter in Ordinary*, London 1988, p. 278, commenting on Newman's understanding of the persons in Trinitarian theology. 'My suggestion is that because, *whatever* our anthropology, we can hardly help hearing the word to mean an "individual intelligent being" we do better to dispense with it.'
[8] John Macmurray, *The Self as Agent*, London, 1957, p. 135.

that activity not simply to be the result of stimulus or awareness, it must be the result of intention. Intentional activity is that which distinguishes the human from the material or the organic. Theoretical activity is the negative aspect of the self in withdrawal from action. Thought which is not directed towards action can become mere phantasy. Reason belongs, for Macmurray, to our capacity to act and only secondarily to our ability to think and reflect.

Macmurray makes clear that we can have either personal or impersonal knowledge. Personal knowledge is given when the other is constituted as a You and an agent. However, it is possible to relate to the other as an object, to withdraw from personal relationships and simply observe and infer, and such a form of relationship forms the basis of the human sciences: 'my conclusions from observation can be true or false, they can be verified or falsified by further observation or by experiment. But it is an abstract knowledge, since it constructs its object by limitation of attention to what is known about other persons without entering into personal relations with them.'[9] The distinction between personal knowledge and impersonal is not an invitation to be caught in the dualism between objective and emotional knowledge. We need to be as much motivated by our emotions in directing our attention in an impersonal manner as we do in a personal manner. In a typically trenchant manner, Macmurray writes, 'But if the scientific state of mind were completely free of emotion, scientific enquiry could not be carried out. It would be entirely motiveless, and therefore impossible.'[10] Emotions and feelings are not, then, to be escaped from as in the Cartesian model of rationality, but rather provide the energy for enquiry.

How are we constituted as persons?

Macmurray gives an example of what it is to be constituted a person by other persons in the simple relationship between a mother and child. In taking the example of the mother and child he also takes a tilt at the Aristotelian tradition which suggests that the human infant is first an animal organism which acquires personality as it grows up. Macmurray says: from the outset the relationship between mother and child is personal;

> in the human infant — and this is the heart of the matter — the impulse to communicate is his sole adaptation to the world in which he is born. Implicit and unconscious it may be, yet it is

---

[9] John Macmurray, *Persons in Relation*, London, 1961, pp. 28-29.
[10] *Ibid.* p. 32.

sufficient to constitute the mother-child relation as the basic
form of human existence, as a personal mutuality, as a "You
and I" with a common life. For this reason the infant is born a
person and not an animal.[11]

The basic motive pattern of the relationship is one of love, but its
negative pole may be, for the infant, fear — the fear of not having
its needs met. Love is directed towards the other, fear towards
oneself, for love needs to be reciprocated. The "You and I" relation
which makes us persons is such that if you act positively towards
me, so offering to enter friendly relationships, and I reject your
advance, I threaten your existence as a person in an absolute
fashion,"[12] and such rejection can be turned to resentment which
is expressed as hatred towards the other, and becomes a dominant
habit. A relationship to the personal Other is primary, and
gradually the infant learns to discriminate between the other
which is personal and that which is impersonal. Because the
primary experiences are personal, it takes time for the child to
discover the impersonal. That is why for some time it will ascribe
personality to favourite impersonal objects; in the task of dis-
crimination tactual perception will be primary. 'In general, the
non personal is that which in action is always means and never
agent.'[13]

The starting point of all knowledge is the reference to the
Personal, and he says:

> any philosophy which finds itself required by its own logic to
> ask the question "How do we know that there are other
> persons?" has refuted itself by a *reductio ad absurdum* and
> should at once revise its original assumptions. For any asser-
> tion — not to speak of any effort of proof — presupposes this
> knowledge by the mere fact that it is communication. If we did
> not know there are other persons we could literally know
> nothing, not even that we ourselves existed.[14]

The motive patterns of love, fear and hatred become the basis for
the distinctions Macmurray makes between different forms of
morality, social philosophy and even Religion, Science and Art. By
concentrating on the mother-child relationship, Macmurray does
not intend to give a biological account of the distinctions but
rather, he says, a clear simple example of the basic motive

[11]   *Ibid*. p. 60.
[12]   *Ibid*. p. 73.
[13]   *Ibid*. p. 82.
[14]   *Ibid*. pp. 16-77.

patterns that occur in all human relationships, though obviously in an increasingly complex form as we develop.

Mother-Child Relation

In our development as persons it is necessary to withdraw from the other. A child, if it is to develop, has to learn to do what its mother has done for it. The mother's refusal throws the child's world into chaos, which heightens its fear and illusion, but enriches its sense of individuality. The child will learn to do what its mother expects, but what is significant for Macmurray is the motive by which it functions.

> The mother's refusal institutes a dichotomy in the child's consciousness between what he expects and what actually occurs; between his demand and the response to it. He is forced into a recognition of the distinction between imagining and perceiving. For what he anticipates in imagination is contradicted by what actually takes place and this institutes the contrast between phantasy and reality.[15]

If there is to be a successful resolution of the conflict between child and mother it will come through some resolution of the child overcoming its fear and perceiving that its mother has not neglected it and still loves it.

> If on the contrary, the child accedes to his mother's demand because he must, and against his will, the tension of the contradiction is not resolved and he remains egocentric and on the defensive; he conforms in behaviour to what is expected of him but as it were, as a matter of policy. In that case he cannot find satisfaction in the new form of co-operation and this remains for him unreal.[16]

Therein are the seeds of dualism in the mind. Faced with a conflict of wills, the child can become a 'good boy' and submit himself to his mother, and create a secret life of phantasy where his wishes are ever granted.

> And this life of the imagination in an imaginary world will be for him his real life in the real world, the world of ideas . . . . He may, however, take the other course. He may seek to impose his will on his mother. He may become a "bad boy", rebellious and aggressive, seeking to gain by force or cunning what is not freely given to him. In that case he will carry the conflict of wills

15 *Ibid.* p. 96.
16 *Ibid.* pp. 102- 103.

into the world of activity and seek power over the Other. When this failure to overcome the negative motivation is established, one or other of these two courses will tend to become habitual by repetition.[17]

Both patterns of behaviour are negative; they destroy the possibility of personal relationships either by making the Other feel she has got to care for him, if we are submissive, or making her afraid if we are aggressive. 'Self interested relation excludes the mutuality it seeks to extort.'[18]

These motive patterns can be fixed in habits and express themselves in morality with a contemplative attitude that is not readily committed to the world, often accepting the *status quo*, but concerned with the satisfactions of an ideal world, or they can be expressed in an aggressive morality such as the law-centred morality of the Stoa and Romans and certain distorted forms of Christianity. The communal motivation will be expressed by hebraic and Christian morality. The social philosophies that flow from the motive patterns are for the aggressive that expressed in the thought of Thomas Hobbes, and the contemplative or submissive in the thought of Rousseau. Always for Macmurray the conception of the person has practical implications.

The Communal Life

For Macmurray religion is the reflective aspect of the community's life. He makes four basic points: first, that no society has existed without religion, proving that its source must lie in some common and universal aspect of human experience. Secondly, that there are no analogues of religion to be found among the higher animals. 'Religion is bound up with that in our experience which makes us persons and not mere organisms.'[19] Thirdly, religion has been the matrix in which all aspects of culture have their root. Fourthly, religion is universal and meant to include all members of society. Religion exists to serve the personal which Macmurray defines as

a universal community of persons in which each cares for all the others, and no one for himself. This ideal of the personal is also the condition of freedom, that is, of full realization of his capacity to act for every person. Short of this, there is unintegrated, and therefore suppressed, negative motivation, there is unresolved fear; and fear inhibits action and destroys freedom.[20]

[17] *Ibid.* pp. 103-104.
[18] *Ibid.* p. 105.
[19] *Ibid.* p. 156.
[20] *Ibid.* p. 159.

The basis of religion lies in the problem of establishing community, but it also celebrates its existence and sustains the intention to maintain it in the future. The intention to maintain community universally has to be expressed symbolically in the idea of a personal Other to which we are all related. This personal Other has to be able to represent our continuity with the community of the past, but also overcome our fear of nature, because life depends on our relationship with the nonpersonal world. Hence the Other is seen as the Creator and the one that can defeat the death which would express the victory of the forces of nature and our isolation from the community of the living. 'The personal must include and subordinate the nonpersonal for the sake of the realization of the personal.'[21] Just as the personal life can be dominated by fear or hatred, so religion can be distorted by negative apperceptions. So:

> if the apperception is pragmatic, the religion will have the form, as it were, of a spiritual technology; an armoury of devices to control the forces which determine practical success or failure, but which are beyond the reach of ordinary human power; a set of ritual devices which placate the hostility or enlist the favour of the divine. If the apperception is contemplative, the religion will be idealist or "purely spiritual". Such religion tends in various manners to be "other worldly", for it is characteristically the representation of an ideal community which is hoped for and imagined but not intended in practice. It is a withdrawal from the world; an escape into phantasy: it offers its symbols not the common world of actual life but away from it to another world which compensates for the unsatisfactory character of the actual.[22]

Besides these distortions, Macmurray shows also how science and art may be accounted for.

> Art and science are derived from religion by a limitation of attention. They are activities of reflection carried on for their own sake, and not for the sake of the personal Other. The one is an activity of emotional reflection, the other of intellectual reflection . . . . The relation of both the artist and the scientist to the world is an impersonal relation. In the critical case which is the relation to their fellow men, they stay aloof. The scientist, intellectually reflective, observes, compares, generalizes and records. The artist contemplates, isolates, particularizes and evaluates, in an activity of emotional reflection.[23]

[21] *Ibid.* p. 165 .
[22] *Ibid.* p. 171.
[23] *Ibid.* p. 176.

Both are forms of rational reflection but they need to be integrated by religion which is the form of personal rational reflection.

What of God?

For Macmurray the traditional proofs for the existence of God are all based on the "I think", and therefore cannot prove the existence of God. Of those proofs he does accept that the argument from design has some cogency. But for Macmurray, God the Other is known in the act of existence; we discover our freedom in relationship with others.

> We live and move and have our being, not in our selves but in one another and what rights or powers or freedom we possess are ours by the grace and favour of our fellowship. Here is the basic fact of our human condition, which we can all know if we stop pretending, and do know in moments when the veil of self-deception is stripped from us and we are forced to look upon our nakedness.[24]

Not only is this the appropriate way to characterize our relationship with each other, but also with the world, as the personal action of God. Matter is subordinate to God's purpose. The traditional way of conceiving the world as a dualism between spirit and matter ends with splitting them asunder. 'The radical objection to dualism is that it denies the "I do" and substitutes on the one hand an "I think", and on the other an "it happens". Action is the integration of knowledge and movement.'[25] The world is to be conceived as God's action which we participate in. Dualism denies the possibility of this integration and verification of this view of relating to the world will be shown in the difference it makes to the lives of those who commit themselves to it.

Criticisms

My criticism of Macmurray will be from a theological perspective.[26] First, is it true that when we examine or reflect upon our natures, we find them orientated towards personal love in the way that Macmurray suggests? We might wish it to be so, but that is a

---

24 *Ibid.* p. 211.
25 *Ibid.* p. 213.
26 Criticism from a psychological perspective may be found in *The Roots of Religion in Biological and Psychological Development in Infancy*. David Maynard, unpublished Cambridge PhD Thesis, in which he points out that personal care is rooted in animal society and not limited to human beings, but rather the result of the extreme dependence of infants due to evolutionary and ecological factors.

different matter. Rather are we not aware of ourselves as a battle ground in which the emotions of hate and fear often appear to have a victory. Very obviously we do establish personal relationships and patterns of sociality, but after Auschwitz is the evidence so clear as to their primacy?

The Christian's confidence in the triumph of the personal is built not simply on his experience of life but on the certainty that comes from the eschatological witness of the Holy Spirit to the significance of the life, death and resurrection of Jesus.

In the introduction to her book *Sartre*, Iris Murdoch comments on:

> Sartre's canonisation of Genet, in which the word "evil" fre-
> quently occurs, seems devoid of any understanding of the
> reality of evil, the nature of cruelty, the harm done to its
> victims, the crippling (for instance, the narrowing of the evil do-
> er's mind) the spreading ripples of misery and further evil
> which evil acts produce.[27]

Does Macmurray show any understanding of the problems poised by such evil? I think not. For Macmurray, evil is clearly the result of the hatred and fear that arise when our love for the other is thwarted. This he regards as probably what is meant by original sin.[28] Such a hatred and fear are begun in relationships with the mother when she appears not to respond to our demands, and despair sets in. How can the situation be resolved? We are told: 'If we may use the language of mature human reflection which, though its content is much richer, has an identical form, the child can only be rescued from his despair by the grace of his mother; by a revelation of her continued love and care which convinces him that his fears are groundless.'[29] This revelation has to come about by an action of the mother.

There are several problems connected with this account. First it does seem that I cannot properly be held responsible for this hatred if my mother chooses not to respond to my demands, if it is part of the necessary process of the Mother withdrawing herself to help the child, as it were, to stand on its own feet. We seem here to be talking about a purely mechanical and automatic process. Secondly, and more tragically, is it not the case that we choose to do evil freely and not out of fear or hatred, but even in the face of love? Thirdly, is the solution simply the revelation of the Mother

---

[27] Iris Murdoch. *Sartre, Romantic Rationalist*, London, 1989, p. 20.
[28] John Macmurray, *Persons in Relation*, London, 1961, p. 75.
[29] *Ibid.* p.90.

continuing to love even by her own action? If we look at this in adult terms, part of the problem is the way our evil acts have the ripple-on effect of which Murdoch writes. How are we to make some kind of reparation; of whom do we ask forgiveness for the wider consequences? It is here, of course, that the believer will want to introduce the God whom we have offended also; but if we continue Macmurray's terms, do we need only a revelation of his love? Do we not need some act that recreates and redeems all that has been ruptured?[30]

It is true that Macmurray describes God 'who is the Creator of the world and the Father of all men. His work in history is the redemption of the world from evil and the setting up of the Kingdom of Heaven.'[31] But from the kind of analogies that Macmurray gives to explain this work, it would seem to be a long way from the classical understanding of atonement by an action of forgiving love that takes upon itself the consequences of the offender's disruption of the moral and created order. Equally, Macmurray has nothing to say about the importance of the offender taking responsibility for his hatred because in Macmurray's explanation there is nothing for which to take responsibility or ask forgiveness. One has simply failed to recognise that one is loved, and that is a *necessary* part of the withdrawal process involved in growing up. When grown up, where then is my responsibility, if in the end all my actions are to be explained in terms dependant upon the way I was brought up by my mother and others?

It is quite clear that Macmurray, by narrowing down the field of the personal to the mutuality of a relationship between mother and child or friends, lays himself open to a considerable number of problems because he fails to unite the personal with the impersonal features of existence. Professor Dorothy Emmet comments on an example given by Macmurray[32] in which the teacher of psychology, in a personal interview with a pupil, becomes suddenly aware that there is something wrong with the pupil. The

---

[30] On the need for objective atonement, see Colin Gunton, *The Actuality of Atonenent*, Edinburgh 1988, who in a chapter on the 'Justice of God' and a discussion of Luther and Paul's views writes: 'The justification of the sinner, then, is only a part to what is meant by the justice of God, which is concerned more broadly in terms of the transformation of the whole created order, as the outcome — as we shall see — of God's loyalty to his creation.' (p. 103).

[31] John Macmurray, *Persons in Relation*, London, 1961, p. 175.

[32] *Ibid.* p. 29.

psychologist switches from the personal relationship to one of treating the pupil as an object of study; the justification for this change being the necessity of helping the pupil. But as Dorothy Emmett points out:

> Throughout, the teacher will have to be practising the difficult art of combining a personal relation to his pupils with the conduct necessary for doing a special job. In relation to a class, it may be necessary to cultivate a certain amount of what Talcot Parsons calls 'affective neutrality'. But a personal relation to his pupils can come through the way he carries out his role. It will not do to speak of behaviour in a role as mechanical or like wearing a mask, and to relegate personal relationships to off duty moments.[33]

Harvey Cox in *The Secular City* argues also for a widening of the understanding of the personal, between Martin Buber's I-Thou and I-It categories. He noted that the church was rooted in what he called a pre-urban ethos 'wanting to promote small town intimacy among urban people and by preaching the necessity of I-Thou relationships as the only ones that are really human.'[34] Instead, said Cox, we need to develop an intermediate concept of the I-You relationship. 'It would include all those public relationships we so enjoy in the city but which we do not allow to develop into private ones.'[35] It is quite clear that Macmurray has no explanation, for example, of relationships with the friendly milkman or postman. More seriously, it is difficult to see that he has much to contribute directly to the moral problems posed by economics and international affairs beyond suggesting they are to serve the personal.

The narrowing down of the personal has also consequences for our relationship with God. We surely have to recognise some kind of asymmetry in our relationship with God. Vincent Brümmer has pointed out both the symmetry and asymmetry involved when we pray for the coming of God's Kingdom and recognise his authority. Clearly it is symmetrical in that both partners have to agree to it personally. But it is clear that the King exercises authority over his subject; equally the subject has to acknowledge the authority, and the King be prepared to accept it.[36] Failing to acknowledge

---

[33] Dorothy Emmet, 'Persons and Community: John Macmurray and Reinhold Niebuhr', a paper given to the HEF Conference, Oxford in March 1984.

[34] Harvey Cox, *The Secular City*, London, 1968, p. 61.

[35] *Ibid.*

[36] Vincent Brümmer, *What are We doing When We pray?* London, p. 52.

this in our relationship with God, means that Macmurray has no room for areas of religious experience which are about facing responsibility and duty. For Macmurray, the fundamental relationship is one of intimate communion. Nicholas Lash puts it well when in *Easter in the Ordinary* he discusses religious experience:

> experiences that matter most ... are at least likely to have the character of responsibility acknowledged, or suffering endured, as they are to have the character of aesthetic satisfaction or heightened feeling. A Christian account of the "experiences that matter most" should be derived from the consideration of the ways in which Jesus came to bear the responsibility of his mission and especially of how it went with him in Gethsemane.[37]

It is quite true that Macmurray talks of our relation with God as one of seeking 'to understand and fulfil his intention',[38] but he has already put a morality that has duty and obligation and law in the category of that which flows from having an aggressive apperception of one relationship with the world and belongs to a morality that comes from the Stoa and Romans.

Leslie Newbigin, in a criticism of Macmurray's earlier work of the thirties[39] points out his failure to appreciate how the Hebrew Torah is to be conceived as God's personal word to his people, and not in any abstract sense of a mechanical law. Newbigin criticised the lack of the idea of obligation in the moral life. Fundamentally, Macmurray lacks any sense of the eschatological tension in the Christian life between the 'yet' and 'not yet' of the final consummation.

> The love of one another does not spring up in us willy-nilly as a result of God's love for us; it passes through by way of the human conscience and will .... Duty, in other words, belongs to the road which Christians must travel, but not to the goal to which they go. Since it concerns what ought to be, but is not yet, it belongs to the world of imperfection: but this does not mean that it can forthwith be discarded by those who have breathed the air of the Kingdom of Heaven in which all Creation shall obey God's will as a long response in which duty need have no place. For it is still the voice of God — but now, not a mere isolated fiat of an unknown will, but part of a whole living communion with a personal God known to us in Christ as infinitely loving.[40]

---

[37] Nicholas Lash, *Easter in Ordinary*, London, 1988, p. 251.
[38] John Macmurray, *Persons in Relation*, London, 1961, p. 217.
[39] Leslie Newbigin, *Christian Freedom in the Modern World*, London, 1937.
[40] *Ibid.* p. 92.

This lack of any sense of eschatological tension also weakens Macmurray's understanding of the nature of religion, and again, I am indebted for Newbigin's pointing this out in Macmurray's earlier work,[41] a weakness which has been carried on into the Gifford Lectures. The problem is that religion for Macmurray is the reflective aspect of the communal experience. It arises out of the need both to face the problems posed in sustaining the communal life it helps to maintain, and celebrates what has been so far achieved. But if religion is meant to be universalised, as Macmurray states, where does such an idea come from? Certainly not from the present experience. So what saves it from the kind of stricture Macmurray has levelled against the form of idealistic religion which is a phantasy resulting from not being able to have one's wishes met in the present? What is surely needed here is the kind of grounding that recognises that the Kingdom has already been established in Christ, but yet remains fully to be consummated. Our celebration and beliefs, then, arise not out of our failures or what we have been able to achieve, but rather out of what God has begun to do and promised to bring to fulfilment.

Equally at the end of the lecture, Macmurray gives a rapid introduction to his conception of God, which is simply the Personal Other by which we can represent our relationships to each other. 'Without the idea of such a universal and personal Other it is impossible to represent the unity of a community of persons each in personal fellowship with all others.'[42]

Leaving aside the obvious criticism that might suggest that Macmurray's God is a product of his own philosophy and that some people do achieve personal relationships and believe in a universal community without the need for God, one is left wondering if the doctrine of the Trinity might have helped him on two counts. First, our relationships with God are all bound to have about them the character of asymmetry. In this world they will never be fully personal because of our own failures and imperfections. How then is God's own personality to be fully grounded and ours if not in some kind of relationship of personal communion within the Godhead, which points surely in the direction of the Trinity understood as a relational being?.

Secondly, Macmurray as we have shown, finds it difficult to unite the personal and impersonal and this extends to the way in which he writes about the impersonal world which he says is subordinate to the personal; we need surely a way of speaking that

---

[41] *Ibid.* p. 55 and following.
[42] John Macmurray, *Persons in Relation*, London, 1961, p. 164.

recognises its own intrinsic value and saves it from the kind of tragic exploitation with which we are so familiar.

Now the doctrine of the Trinity speaks also of the Second Person uniting himself to the world in the human nature of Jesus, in such a way that all things are brought into a fresh unity with Cod. Kallistos Ware writes:

> In God's original plan humanity was intended to act as a mediator and priest, to unify the creation and offer it back to God. But instead of doing this, we humans have produced disharmony, not unity, within ourselves and between the world and God. Christ, the son of God, has therefore come as true man to fulfil the task of mediation that we have left undone. Jesus Christ, the God-man, the *Theanthropos*, is the mediator. In his person created things are summed up and recapitulated (Eph. 1: 10): he draws them all together, holds them all in unity (Col: 17), and offers them all back to the Father. This work of cosmic mediation, inaugurated by Jesus Christ as 'head' (Col.1:18) is continued and extended by each member of Christ's Body the church.[43]

We may want to say something about this work going on outside the Church, and the failure of the Church in its task. But clearly Ware finds in the Greek Fathers a way of unifying the personal and impersonal which is more in the way of mediation, of drawing things together, than subordination. He describes the vocation of man thus:

> It is our vocation, then not only to unify ourselves and the world around us, not only to hold together the material and the spiritual and to express them as an undivided whole, reaching out beyond created limits, we are also to unite ourselves and the world to God, and so divinise creation.[44]

However despite these criticisms which show Macmurray's failure adequately to account for the way in which the impersonal and personal aspects of our lives interpenetrate, it is clear that Macmurray has made a significant contribution to a fuller understanding of the nature of the person.[45]

---

[43] Kallistos Ware, 'The Unity of the Human Person according to the Greek Fathers', *Persons and Personality*, edited by A. Peacocke and G. Gillet, Oxford, 1987, p.102.

[44] *Ibid.* p. 199.

[45] See for example Adrian Thatcher, 'Christian Theism and the Concept of a Person', *ibid.* p. 181, also *The Forgotten Trinity, The Report of The BCC Study Commission on Trinitarian Doctrine Today*, London, 1989, p. 19. Both see Macmurray as offering an alternative to Western individualism.

Firstly against the dualistic divisions of soul and body, mind and matter, the self as subject and the self as object, Macmurray affirms a unity given in intentional action and moreover an action that is directed towards mutuality. Too often the foregoing dualisms have diminished our understanding of human experience and relationships, particularly the way in which the self has been seen as the locus of freedom and the only originator of values over against a determined and valueless world. This in turn has led to patterns of human behaviour in which the other is to be determined or exploited by force.

Secondly Macmurray states the primacy of relational being. We are first persons. Personality against many modern conceptions is not achieved in isolation from or at the expense of others or by the development of certain faculties such as reason, or by the conscious social acceptance of others. We simply cannot exist or be ourselves apart from others. We are simply created to be directed outwards in intentional activity to mutuality or friendship or communion (all used by Macmurray to describe the state of relational being).

Other people are no longer there to be feared or dominated but rather to sustain and constitute us in mutual loving and be sustained and constituted in turn. Macmurray's views have considerable implications for a world in which we lament a selfish individualism that destroys human community or a consumer collectivism in which the individual is simply lost. We are made for community rather than individualism or collectivism, with all that that implies for social ethics.

If we ask what are the sources of Macmurray's thought about the person then we can recognise the attachment to St John's Gospel in his work and the theme of friendship found there and the manner in which way Father and Son are mutually related but also distinctive. [46] In his book *The Search for Reality in Religion* he relates how he was brought up in a deeply religious environment in which Calvin's *Institutes* were openly studied by his father, and how at one time he seriously considered being a missionary. Thomas Torrance has noted in the Reformed tradition of Scotland how

> the notion of the person is held to be controlled by the person constituting and person - intensifying activity of God in the Incarnation, such that union with Christ becomes the ground

[46] See the allusions to John's Gospel in *The Clue to History,* London, 1938, and much later in the lectures *Ye My Friends* and *To Save From Fear,* London, 1979.

for interpersonal relations in the Church. Relations between persons have ontological force and are part of what persons are as persons — they are real, person constituting relations.[47]

Though Macmurray saw doctrine in a negative manner, we should not underestimate the probable unconscious effect of worship and the Reformed tradition in which he was brought up upon his thought.

A.J. Ayer, who succeeded Macmurray to the Grote Chair at University College, disparagingly noted that Macmurray brought from Balliol College Oxford where he had been a Fellow the missionary spirit of Jowett, and Macmurray's interests being in ethics and politics he liked to preach his doctrines outside academic circles.[48] But then, as I have noted in this paper, Macmurray passionately believed that philosophy and religion were to do with the whole of experience and have profound implications for the way we live. I hope I have succeeded in suggesting that this is still true of his thought, particularly with regard to his understanding of the person; and the passion of the preacher and the commitment of the missionary may well be necessary in the telling of something so important.

---

[47] Thomas Torrance's *Transformation and Convergence in the Frame of Knowledge*, Belfast 1984, p. 230.

[48] A. J. Ayer, *More of My Life,* Oxford, 1984, p. 16.

III

Theological Theses

1. Human Being As Relational Being
Twelve Theses for a Christian Anthropology[1]

Christoph Schwöbel

1.   The understanding of human being as relational being forms a common element in contemporary anthropological reflection.

Contemporary anthropological reflection is represented in a wide variety of forms. However diverse the different approaches may seem at first sight, there nevertheless seems to be a basic common element in most forms of anthropological thought and research. It consists in the understanding of human being as relational being. Since modern anthropology largely abandoned the view of the distinctiveness of humanity in terms of the possession of a substantial soul, human being has come to be understood from its relational structure.[2] Most of the relationships in which human beings exist have in this way become the basis for attempts at determining what it means to be human. In biological approaches the relationship of human beings to other parts of the animal world and to its common microbiological

---

[1]   This paper was first discussed at the weekly research seminar of the Research Institute in Systematic Theology in November 1988. Its intention is to suggest a basic outline for the project of Christian anthropology centred on the notion of human being as relational being by mapping out some of the central tenets of anthropology in the framework of Christian dogmatics. The original form of presentation in a series of theses has been maintained for publication in this volume. To offer a detailed argument for the over-all conception and for particular steps in the exposition would require a far more exhaustive treatment.

[2]   cf. Wolfhart Pannenberg, *Anthropology in Theological Perspective*. Translated by Matthew J. O'Connell, Edinburgh: T.&T. Clark 1985, pp. 27-42.

structures is employed as the chosen route for describing the status of human being in the natural order. In this way the relationship to the world in which human beings live in virtue of their bodily existence is perceived as the determinative factor for human nature. In other approaches, the social dimension of human life, the fact that human beings exist in specific societal relations to other human beings, is seen as the dominant feature for any attempt at determining the structure and destiny of human existence. Other forms of anthropological research see the cultural existence of human beings as the highway for understanding human beings as beings that are by nature cultural beings. Here the creation of symbolic systems of communication that regulate the relationship of human beings to the natural world and their forms of social organisation is understood as the focal point from which the relational existence of humanity should be viewed.

In contrast to these empirical approaches which concentrate on the relationship of human beings to nature, the social form of their existence or the cultural shaping of all human relatedness, some schools of thought have concentrated on the reflexive relationship in which the human person can become the subject as well as the object of reflection. This self-relation is then interpreted as the transcendental condition for the possibility of all empirical attempts at finding the characteristics of human being in its natural, social or cultural relatedness. This capacity for self-reflection, which is documented in anthropological reflection itself, is claimed to be the distinctive feature of the human condition that determines all social and cultural relations.

These different approaches from one specific set of relations can be employed either in a reductionist or in a non-reductionist way. A reductionist interpretation claims that the dominant relational dimension that forms the basis for this approach is the only dimension of human being in the sense that all other dimensions have to be explained as specific developments from the fundamental dimension. While a reductionist analysis is basically one-dimensional, a non-reductionist analysis has to retain a multi-dimensional view of human relatedness, but can nevertheless claim that one specific relation in which human beings exist forms the perspective from which to interpret the others.

2.   The distinctive thesis of Christian theological anthropology is that human being as relational being is rooted in the relationship of the triune God to humanity.

Christian theological anthropology does not present an exception to the relational view of human being that seems to be dominant in modern anthropological reflection. In fact, Christian theologians have in recent years done much to establish this view as a fundamental perspective for anthropology.[3] Yet, theological anthropology — obsolete as ever in the eyes of its critics — does not subscribe to the view that human being as relational being can be adequately and completely understood from the immanent relations of human beings to themselves, to other persons and to the cultural and natural world where transcendence appears only in the form of the self-transcendence of human existence. Christian Anthropology does not only claim that the relationship of humanity to transcendence is the dominant perspective from which all the other relationships should be understood. It claims, more specifically, that the relationship of God to humanity is the key to the understanding of all relationships in which human beings exist, including humanity's relationship to God.[4] But even more than that, it asserts that the relationship of God to humanity can only be adequately understood as the basis for human relational being, if it is understood as the relationship of the triune God, Father, Son and Spirit to humanity.

[3] cf. Eberhard Jüngel, 'Der Gott entsprechende Mensch. Bemerkungen zur Gottebenbildlichkeit des Menschen als Grundfigur theologischer Anthropologie' (1975) in: Eberhard Jüngel, *Entsprechungen: Gott-Wahrheit-Mensch. Theologische Erörterungen*, Munich: Chr. Kaiser 1980, pp. 290-321. — Wilfried Härle, 'Die Rechtfertigungslehre als Grundlegung der Anthropologie', in: W. Härle/E. Herms, *Rechtfertigung. Das Wirklichkeitsverständnis des christlichen Glaubens*. Göttingen: Vandenhoeck & Ruprecht 1980, pp. 78-100. — Ingolf U. Dalferth/Eberhard Jüngel, 'Person und Gottebenbildlichkeit', in: *Christlicher Glaube in moderner Gesellschaft 24*, Freiburg/Basel/Wien: Herder 1981, pp. 57-99. — Thomas F. Torrance, 'The Goodness and Dignity of Man in the Christian Tradition', *Modern Theology* 4 (1988), pp. 308-322, esp. pp. 311ff.

[4] Cf. Dalferth/Jüngel, op. cit. pp. 60-64. Richard Norris has recently pointed out that the distinctive characteristic of a scriptural anthropology is not a systematic anthropological conception, but the specific way in which human life is lived as determined by God's relationship to his creation. 'The scriptural "way of talking" about human beings is, then, systematically *theological* in the sense that human individuals are identified and understood as such through their relationship to God. Their being, to use one of Luther's favourite phrases, is *coram Deo*. "God" is the name of the ultimate context in which and to which they are responsive.' R. Norris, 'Human Being', in *Keeping the Faith. Essays to Mark the Centenary of* Lux Mundi (ed. Geoffrey Wainwright), London: SPCK 1989, pp. 78-98. p. 80.

This has a number of crucial implications for the project of a Christian theological anthropology. First of all, the view that all human being as relational being can only be understood from God's relationship to humanity applies not only to the ontological constitution of humanity, but also to the way in which human beings can come to acquire knowledge of their ontological constitution. In the Christian tradition there is a strong strand that claims that humanity has an implicit or explicit, but ambiguous awareness of God's existence (*notitia*), but that unambiguous knowledge of God, and specifically knowledge of God's relationship to humanity (*cognitio Dei et cognitio hominis*) is only possible on the basis of God's relationship to us in the revelation of the Father through the Son, in the Spirit.[5] On this view, the revelation of God in Christ is the foundation for what it means to be human. This implies, secondly, that the true humanity of Christ is understood as the paradigm for true knowledge of human being. If Christ as the Second Adam is seen as the paradigm of what it means to be human, this means that the true pattern for understanding human being is not the factual existence of humanity, but the new humanity of Christ in whom humanity is recreated and restored. From the perspective constituted by God's self-disclosure in Christ the true humanity of Christ becomes the basis for understanding the created destiny of humanity as well as the human contradiction of this destiny and its recreation in Christ. This perspective of interpretation therefore comprehends the traditional distinction between human existence *in statu*

---

[5] The *locus classicus* for the significance of this distinction for knowledge of God and of ourselves is, of course, Calvin's discussion in the first book of the *Institutes of the Christian Religion* (tr. Ford Lewis Battles, Philadelphia: The Westminster Press 1960). Cf. the stimulating discussion in Iain Paul, *Knowledge of God. Calvin, Einstein and Polanyi*, Edinburgh: Scottish Academic Press 1987, pp. 1-38; cf. also Thomas F. Torrance, 'Knowledge of God and Speech about him according to John Calvin', in *Theology in Reconstruction*, London: SCM Press, pp. 76-98. For Luther's use of the *cognitio Dei et hominis* formula cf. Gerhard Ebeling, 'Cognitio Dei et hominis', in: G. Ebeling, *Lutherstudien* vol.I, Tübingen: J. C. B. Mohr 1971, pp. 221-72. A comprehensive account of the debate concerning awareness of God's existence and knowledge of God's relationship to us can be found in Carl Heinz Ratschow, *Lutherische Dogmatik zwischen Reformation und Aufklärung*, Vol. II, Gütersloh: Gütersloher Verlagshaus Gerd Mohn 1966, pp. 29-58. For an illuminating discussion which leads, however, to quite different conclusions cf. Wolfhart Pannenberg, *Systematische Theologie* vol.I, Göttingen: Vandenhoeck & Ruprecht 1988, pp. 121-132.

integritatis as well as in *statu corruptionis* and in *statu gratiae*.[6] This approach has, thirdly, significant consequences for the method of Christian theological anthropology. On this view, adequate and complete knowledge of what it means to be human can neither be read off the empirical findings of the different anthropological disciplines, nor developed from the reflexive character of human self-consciousness. Neither a strategy of theological reinterpretation of non-theological anthropological theories, nor of accepting these theories as bases for anthropological understanding to which theology then adds its special Christian interpretation would seem to be capable of doing justice to the principle that adequate knowledge of what it means to be human is dependent on God's relation to humanity in revelation. Therefore, the relationship of theological anthropology to non-theological anthropologies should not so much be seen in terms of a possible (theological) synthesis, but in terms of a dialogue.[7]

3. *Faith as it is grounded in the revelation of God the Father through the Son in the Spirit is the form of life where the relationship of God to humanity is acknowledged and appropriated as the foundation of human being as relational being and as the condition of the possibility of adequate relational existence.*

It would be a contradiction against the relational character of human existence, if theology were to claim to be able to view God's relationship to humanity from the standpoint of God. The relationship of God to humanity as it constitutes human being as relational being and as it is disclosed in God's self-revelation is only accessible from the perspective of faith, where God's relationship to humanity is acknowledged as the foundation of human relational being. Faith as the human response to God's revelation can be characterised as a relationship of absolute trust in God,

---

6 For this classical distinction and its relevance for contemporary Christian anthropology cf. Hans-Georg Fritzsche, *Lehrbuch der Dogmatik, Teil III: Christologie*, Berlin: Evangelische Verlagsanstalt 1975, pp. 13-97.

7 This indicates my criticism of Pannenberg's attempt to provide a foundation for Christian anthropology in general anthropological studies. Cf. my article 'Theology in Anthropological Perspective?' *King's Theological Review* 10 (1989), pp. 21-25. Pannenberg's *Anthropology* remains the most comprehensive attempt to develop a theological anthropology in the context of contemporary reflection in the human sciences.

Father, Son and Spirit. I have argued elsewhere that in confessions of faith the conditions for the possibility of the *act* of faith are confessed as the *content* of faith.[8] Faith can therefore be interpreted as a specific ordered relationship of certainty, truth and reality. The certainty of faith is constituted by the inspiration of the Spirit which enables us to accept and acknowledge the truth of God's revelation in Christ as the disclosure of his true relationship to his creation. The truth on which faith relies is constituted by God's self-revelation in the Son which discloses the true relationship of God to his creation as saving love. Therefore the truth of faith as it is grounded in God's self-revelation does not only concern one aspect of reality, but refers to the constitution of all reality through God's creative love.

This threefold passive constitution of faith refers to God's relationship to humanity as the condition for the possibility of faith as the active relationship of humanity to God which is the adequate response to God's relationship to his creation. Faith as the basic orientation of human life which is in accordance with God's relationship to humanity implies a view of reality as constituted by God's creative action and as disclosed in his revelation. It provides therefore the framework in terms of which an adequate understanding of what it means to be human is to be developed.[9] Human being as relational being is seen as constituted and determined by God's relationship to the world and to humanity. The relationships in which human beings exist to themselves, to other persons, to nature and to culture are constituted by and have their criterion of adequacy in God's relationship to the world.

---

[8] Cf. C. Schwöbel, 'Die Rede vom Handeln Gottes im christlichen Glauben. Beiträge, zu einem systematisch-theologischen Rekonstruktionsversuch', in: W. Härle, R. Preul (eds.), *Vom Handeln Gottes. Marburger Jahrbuch Theologie I*, Marburg: N. G. Elwert 1987, pp. 56-81, especially pp. 61-64.

[9] In English theology this emphasis on the fundamental relationship of faith as the constitution of the human person is clearly developed in Henry Scott Holland's essay 'Faith' in *Lux Mundi. Studies in the Religion of the Incarnation* (ed. Charles Gore), London: John Murray 1889 (5th edn. 1890). For a stimulating discussion of the implications of such an approach cf. the essays in both volumes published in commemoration of *Lux Mundi*: Stephen Sykes, 'Faith', in *Keeping the Faith* (n.4), pp. 1-24 and Robert Morgan: 'Faith', in *The Religion of the Incarnation*. Anglican Essays in Commemoration of Lux Mundi, Bristol: Bristol Classical Press 1989, pp. 132.

4.   Faith is the eschatological existence of New Being for humanity.

Faith is, however, not only *epistemologically* constitutive for a Christian theological anthropology, insofar as it provides the framework in which a theological understanding of what it means to be human can be developed. It is much more than that. Faith is *ontologically* the mode of being in which human beings actualize their relational being in accordance with God's relationship to humanity. This requires further explication. We have above referred to the passive constitution of faith in God's trinitarian action. Insofar as faith is passively constituted in God's action, it has the ontological status of all *created* being as not being self-produced, but created by the creative agency of God. Insofar as faith is the active personal response to God's action in constituting certainty concerning the truth of the revelation of his relation to reality, it has the specific ontological status of the *personal* existence that is the distinction of human beings in creation.

Faith can be characterized as eschatological existence since it is the appropriate human response to God's relationship to his creation. It is participation in the relationship of humanity to God which is the purpose of God's will for his creation. Therefore it is characterized by eschatological ultimacy. The warrant of this eschatological ultimacy is the truth of the Gospel of God's self-disclosure through the Son in the Spirit which cannot be surpassed. This is the element of truth in all conceptions of realized eschatology. But insofar as the truth of the Gospel is not yet universally evident, so that God's relationship to humanity is not yet universally disclosed as the foundation of the human relationship to God and the world, faith remains distinct from hope. And this is the element of truth in all conceptions of future-oriented eschatology. The difference between faith and hope is, however, not a difference in content, but with regard to the present particularity and future universality of God's self-disclosure.

Faith as the distinctive mode of being that is made possible by the action of the triune God, Father, Son and Spirit sees love as the fundamental attribute of God's being and therefore as the basic pattern for the interpretation of the relationship of God to his creation. Because Christian faith understands its own being as constituted by God's creative, reconciling and creative love, the love of God becomes the fundamental guideline for meaning and orientation in the world. It is the conviction of faith of God's love as the ultimate determinative principle of everything there is that defines the content of Christian hope. Faith, love and hope are therefore the ultimate principles for a Christian ontology.

In our thesis we have characterized the eschatological exist-ence of faith with Paul Tillich's concept of New Being. This indicates, on the one hand, the ontological status of faith which is not only knowledge about an ontological state, but which has epistemic character in virtue of its ontological status. On the other hand, it indicates that the being of faith is not simply to be identified with our factual existence. It is the being of new humanity in Christ grounded in the reconciliation of God and humanity in Christ which is the condition for the possibility of true relational human being. Following Tillich, we can understand the novelty of New Being in three interrelated senses.[10] First of all, it is new in the sense of being *creatively* new, insofar as the true relationship between God and humanity is not a stage in the natural development of humanity. It is grounded in the rela-tionship of God the creator to his creation. Secondly, it is new in the sense of being the *reconstitution*, the renewal of the relation-ship between God and humanity which God intended from the beginning. New Being in Christ should therefore not be under-stood as God's second attempt in establishing a relationship to humanity in which he makes up for the failure of his first attempt. And thirdly, New Being is new in the sense of being the *fulfilment* of the relationship between God and humanity. The New Being which is established and revealed in God's recon-ciliation with humanity in Christ is not subject to being surpassed by an even newer form of Being. It is eschatologically ultimate Being. Whatever advances into novelty and whatever creative transformations the *eschaton* will bring, they will not make the appearance of New Being in Jesus Christ obsolete.

5. *The life of faith is characterized by the overcoming of the contradiction of sin through God's justifying grace and by the acknowledgement of human createdness.*

In the Christian tradition the opposite of faith is not unbelief, but sin. This illustrates once more that faith is not to be regarded exclusively as an epistemic attitude, but as a basic orientation of life. As the opposite of faith sin is to be interpreted not primarily

---

[10] Cf. Paul Tillich, 'Das Neue Sein als Zentralbegriff einer christlichen Theologie', in: *Mensch und Wandlung. Eranos Jahrbuch* 23 (1955), pp. 251-274, also in *Gesammelte Werke* vol. VIII, pp. 220-239.

as an offence committed against a law, as the transgression of a commandment. It is primarily the violation of a relationship, the relationship between God the creator and his human creatures. As the story of the Fall indicates, the temptation to sin consists in the revolt against the limitations implied in the relationship of creator and creature in order to assume the sovereignty of God the creator. In the attempt at assuming the divine prerogative of knowledge of good and evil, the knowledge of the creator whose goodness is the only standard of goodness, human beings abuse their finite freedom to respond to the creator in gratitude and obedience in order to grasp his sovereign and infinite freedom.[11] The narrative graphically illustrates how this violation of the relationship between God and his creatures does not only distort their relationship to God — the source of their being becomes a threat to their existence — but also mars the relationship between the sexes, the relationship of human beings to their bodily existence and their relationship to nature.[12] In the Fall human beings have dislocated themselves in the relational order of created being. Dislocation produces disorientation. In trying to put themselves in the place of the creator they do not relate to their own relatedness in accordance with its created structure, but in contradiction to it. Therefore sin is not only self-deception, but also self-contradiction insofar as by sinning human beings contradict their own destiny in the created order.

The fate of sin is from the human perspective irreparable dislocation. Human beings remain relational beings bound into the order of relatedness which is the structure of created being, but they lose their ability to relate to God, to themselves, to other persons and to nature in accordance with the intrinsic order of relatedness. Sin does not create a new reality, but it forces human beings to relate to reality in a way that contradicts its created order. As the narrative of the Fall indicates, sin has not only the character of a sinful act, it also becomes the fate for the

---

[11] For this understanding of divine goodness cf. my article 'God's Goodness and Human Morality', *Nederlands Theologisch Tijdschrift* 43 (1989), pp. 122-138.

[12] One of the most perceptive discussions of the Fall is Charles Williams' essay 'The Myth of the Alteration in Knowledge', in *He Came Down from Heaven*, London: Faber & Faber 1950, pp. 17-28. Williams explains the temptation of sin as 'the wish to know an antagonism in the good, to find out what the good would be like if a contradiction were introduced into it' (p. 20). The difference introduced in the Fall consists in the 'mode of knowledge' (p. 21) and this is characterized as 'the entrance of contradiction in the spirit' (p. 22). I am grateful to my colleague Dr. Brian Horne for bringing this to my attention.

whole of humanity. It has this fateful character, because human beings do not have the ability to restore their relationship to God the creator by their own means. To ascribe this ability to human beings would mean acribing to them the power of God the creator — and this would be the ultimate vindication of sin.[13] The doctrine of original sin gives powerful expression to the fact that the broken relationship with God cannot be restored by human effort, indeed, every effort to attempt this participates in the character and fate of sin.

The perspective of faith is defined by the central promise of the Christian Gospel that God has restored his relationship to human beings in Christ, so that human beings are in virtue of the reconciling work of the Son and in the power of the Spirit enabled to respond to God's relationship to humanity in faith. Reformation theology has expressed this restoration of the relationship of humanity to God in the concept of justification. This expresses the two fundamental elements of reconciliation, i.e. that it is God's judgement over sin and that the sinner is pronounced righteous. This forensic understanding of justification is intended to fend off an understanding of reconciliation as a substantial change from being a sinner to being saved, because that would imply that the one who is judged is not the one who is justified. This understanding of justification should, however, not be played off against the reality of righteousness. The one who is pronounced righteous is thus made righteous. Luther has applied the concept of justification as the summary expression of the relationship between God and humanity to the anthropological question by claiming that being justified by faith is the definition of what it means to be human: 'Paulus... breviter hominis definitionem colligit, dicens Hominem justificari fide.'[14]

---

[13] Cf. Wilfried Härle's precise exposition of the fact that Christian faith emphasizes the accountability and responsibility of human beings for sin while at the same time denying the possibility of ascribing the overcoming of sin to human agency, Härle op. cit. (note 3) pp. 94ff.

[14] M. Luther, *Disputatio de homine 1536*, WA 39/1, p. 176, 33-35. Eberhard Jüngel has followed Luther in the Pauline emphasis that justification is the event in which human being is brought into correspondence with God through the being of Jesus Christ. 'Justification' expresses in this sense the ontological definition of human being in God. Cf. 'Der Gott entsprechende Mensch', op. cit. (note 3) pp. 298f. Wilfried Härle and Eilert Herms have even more fundamentally developed the concept of justification as the exposition of the view of reality of Christian faith. In the framework of this approach Wilfried Härle has presented Christian anthropology as grounded in justification-faith. This, however, implies that 'justification' does not denote a

One central aspect of this understanding of justification as the overcoming of the contradiction of sin is that it implies that justification restores humanity to a non-contradictory relationship with God and the world. The justification of the sinner puts an end to the dislocation of humanity as the result of their attempt at assuming God's place in creation, and relocates humanity in its relationship to God and to the world. In this sense the justification of sinful humanity is the restoration of human createdness which is acknowledged in faith. Faith therefore implies the acknowledgement that human being as relational being is in all its relations dependent on God's relationship to humanity and the world. This is the condition for overcoming the disorientation of sin through the new orientation of faith. This new orientation of faith is based on the restoration of the relationship between God and humanity which is acknowledged by fundamental trust in God as the ground and end of all created existence.

6. In faith the destiny of humanity to live as created in the image of God is recreated as life in the image of Christ.

It is the specific distinction of humanity to share not only in the ontological status of createdness with the whole creation, but to have a specific destiny in being created in the image of God. After the Fall the image of God can no longer be read off from the factual existence of human beings. The dislocation of human beings in the created cosmos and their subsequent disorientation does not permit an unambiguous distinction between what in human

---

particular stage in the *ordo salutis* and consequently one aspect of soteriology among others, but designates, following the Reformers, the comprehensive self-interpretation of Christian faith. The attempt to interpret the doctrine of justification as the fundamental article of faith that determines the understanding of all the other articles in the Creed underlies Martin Kähler's dogmatics *Die Wissenschaft von der christlichen Lehre*, Erlangen 1883. Carl Heinz Ratschow has recently developed this approach in the context of the dialogue of religions in order to show that 'justification' is the 'diacritical principle' that distinguishes Christianity from non-Christian religions. Cf. 'Rechtfertigung. Diakritisches Prinzip des Christentums im Verhältnis zu anderen Religionen', in: *Von den Wandlungen Gottes. Beiträge zur systematischen Theologie*, Berlin/New York: de Gruyter 1986, pp. 336-375.

existence is indicative of the created destiny of humanity and
what documents the fate of sin. The relational understanding of
human being and the relational interpretation of sin furthermore
challenges all attempts to specify which substantive parts of
humanity, like reason, could have remained unaffected in the
Fall. Since the relationship of humanity to God is the fundamental
relationship which determines the whole being of humanity in all
its relationships and in all its aspects, the contradiction against
this relationship affects the whole relational being of humanity.

The perspective from which the created destiny of humanity to
live as the image of God can be known, is therefore the perspective
of faith as the eschatological existence of New Being which is
grounded in the restoration of the relationship between God and
humanity through God's justifying grace in Christ. For this
reason the image of Christ is the only way in which human beings
are enabled to recognise their created destiny as the image of
God.[15] God's self-disclosure in Christ the second Adam is therefore
the only access for the recognition of the created destiny for the
first Adam. The image of God in the first Adam as the created
destiny of humanity before the contradiction of sin is only accessible
to us in the image of Christ in whom the contradiction of sin is
overcome. The humanity of Christ is therefore the pattern for
rediscovering the image of God.

The humanity of Christ is not to be understood simply as the
possession of a human 'nature' so that Christ according to his
human nature is a member of the natural kind designated by the
concept 'humanity'. This would mean to understand the humanity
of Christ in terms of a preconception of what it means to be human
whose paradigm is the factual, i.e. sinful, state of humanity.
Theologically this would mean to subject the appearance of New
Being in Christ to the criteria of 'old being', to understand
humanity as it appears *remoto Christo*. This is clearly incompatible with the approach of theological anthropology from the
perspective of faith. For theological anthropology the definition of
humanity is not derived from a 'natural' stereotype of what it
means to be human, but from the revelation of true humanity in

---

[15] For a consistently *christofocal* interpretation of creation in the image
of God cf. Philip Edgcumbe Hughes, *The True Image. The Origin and
Destiny of Man in Christ*, Leicester/Grand Rapids: Inter-Varsity
Press/W. B. Eerdmans 1989.

the humanity of Christ which in this way becomes the criterion for assessing any natural understanding of human 'nature'.[16]

What then is the distinctive character of the humanity of Christ that makes it the definitive revelation of what it means to be human in the perspective of faith? In the biblical witness to the revelation of God in Christ, the distinctive features of the humanity of Christ do not only consist in the fact that he participates in the relationships that characterise human being as relational being, insofar as it is passively constituted by the relationship of God to humanity and subject to the conditions of created existence in its relationship to nature and culture. And it is not only characterized by the ability to relate actively to these relationships, to respond to the relationship of God to humanity in obedience and love or in contradiction and disobedience. Its distinctive characteristic is rather that the humanity of Christ is the perfect human response to God so that God's relationship to humanity is not answered as in the first Adam by revolt and disobedience, but by obedience and love. Where the first Adam abuses his finite freedom to contradict the relationship of God to humanity and to reject his created destiny, the second Adam uses his finite freedom to correspond in his relationship to God to God's relationship to humanity, by yielding to the calling of the Spirit and by doing the will of the Father, and thereby he fulfils the destiny of being the image of God. Where the image of God is restored in the relation of humanity to God, all the other relationships in which humanity exist are restored as well, the relationship to other persons is restored in the community of disciples and nature becomes the place for the experience of healing and beauty.

7.   *The conformity with Christ in faith through the justification of the sinner is the complete definition of the human person.*

The way in which human beings participate in the restored image of God in Christ is not by trying to imitate the image of Christ as the pattern for redeemed humanity (*imitatio Christi*), but by being conformed to the humanity of Christ in faith by God's

---

[16] Cf. Dalferth/Jüngel op. cit. pp. 78-84; cf. also the extensive technical discussion in I. U. Dalferth, 'Homo definiri nequit. Logisch-philosophische Bemerkungen zur theologischen Bestimmung des Menschen', *Zeitschrift für Theologie und Kirche* 76 (1979), pp. 191-224.

justifying grace (*conformitas Christi*).[17] This means not to see Christ as the example of the restored image of God that we have to emulate, but to accept Christ as the disclosure of God's true relationship to humanity and humanity's true relationship to God. The conformity with Christ is the result of a disclosure-experience which comprises three constitutive elements: the acknowledgement that the reality of my life apart from Christ mirrors the dislocation and disorientation of relational being in the state of sin; the recognition that in Christ the divine - human relationship is restored in the self-disclosure of God's relationship to humanity and in the revelation of the true relationship of humanity to God; and the active acknowledgement that the truth of the revelation in Christ is the effective recreation of human relational being and human personhood in my life, so that I am relocated in the relationship between God and the world and receive the true orientation of my life in Christ. Conformity with Christ is the pattern of relational being in the image of Christ as participation in the eschatological existence of New Being.

The claim that conformity with Christ is the true definition of the human person in the image of God has a number of crucial corollaries. First of all, the character of human personhood is not primarily determined by the relationship of humanity to non-personal and non-human nature, because it is not the relationship of humanity to nature that is the determinative relationship of human being, but the relationship to God. Therefore any attempt at grounding the definition of human personhood on a comparison with non-personal nature is necessarily incomplete, and becomes false if it is claimed to be complete. Secondly, the attempt to derive the character of human personhood from the reflection on inter-personal human relationships or on intra-personal self-reflection is also ambiguous, because from the perspective of faith all social and reflexive relations of the human person reflect the dislocation and disorientation of sin. Thirdly, the understanding of personhood based on the conformity with Christ in faith remains incomplete unless it is developed in its full trinitarian sense.

---

[17] Cf. O. Tarvainen, 'Der Gedanke der Conformitas Christi in Luther's Theologie', *Zeitschrift für Systematische Theologie* 22 (1953), pp. 26-43. Thomas à Kempis' teaching on the *imitatio Christi* certainly emphasised the priority of God in the divine-human relationship and offered a radical redefinition of nature and grace which is centred on the primacy of grace. Yet the notion of merit does not seem to be completely excluded. The *conformitas Christi*, on the other hand, stresses that the believer is conformed to Christ so that Christ fulfils the works of the law in the believer.

In Christian faith Christ is confessed as true God and true man. He is true God in the specific sense of being the Son of God, the second person of the Trinity, insofar as his person is constituted by his relationship to the Father and to the Spirit. He is true man, insofar as in him true humanity is recreated as the adequate response of humanity to God, Father, Son and Spirit. These are, however, not two modes of being that are separately exemplified in his person. Jesus Christ as the one incarnate Son is who he is insofar as his person is constituted through the unique relationship of the Father and the Spirit to him which is the condition for his responding relationship to the Spirit and the Father in the relationships of his human life. In the unity of his person Jesus Christ is for us the revelation of God's relationship to us in the relationship of Jesus Christ, the incarnate Son, to the Father and the Spirit. Being conformed to Christ through God's justifying grace in faith means therefore to be conformed to Jesus Christ's relationship to the Father and the Spirit. The conformity with Christ implies participating through the gift of the Spirit in the relationship of the Son to the Father. Through the Son and in the Spirit we are enabled to enter as God's daughters and sons into relationship with the Father. At this point, however, a number of important distinctions have to be made. Whereas the relationship of Father, Son and Spirit is immediate and direct, our relationship to the Father is mediated through the Son and in the Spirit. We would not be able to participate in this relationship without Christ the mediator, and it is through faith in Christ that we are enabled to participate in his relationship to the Father.

If conformity with Christ is seen as the full definition of the human person, this means that the person of Christ becomes the focus for the definition of the human person insofar as in him the image of God is restored and disclosed for us as the image of Christ. The understanding of the human person is in this way defined through the relationship of the human person to the tripersonal God in Christ. Does this imply that the concept of the person characterizes the relational being of humanity in analogy to the relational being of God in the persons of Father, Son and Spirit? It is at this point that utmost theological caution is called for. If this meant that the analogy involved here were understood as the *analogia entis*, it would lead to the well known difficulties of positing the concept of being as a *tertium comparationis* between humanity and God which would contradict the fundamental truth that all being is the result of God's creative and sustaining agency. Barth's counter-proposal of understanding the analogy as the *analogia fidei* could be accepted as more adequate, if faith is not only understood epistemologically as the mode in which we perceive the analogy between God's relational being and human relational being, but ontologically as the way in which human relational being is constituted and restored through the relationship of the trinitarian God to humanity. This is, however, only possible, if the analogy between the trinitarian persons and the human person is strictly interpreted as an *analogia transcendentalis*, both in its ontological and in its epistemological sense. The trinitarian God is the condition for the being of human persons as well as the condition for knowledge of the truth about the being of the human person.

This view of the definition of the human person as conformity with Christ in faith through the relationship to the tri-personal God has conceptual as well as ontological implications. The most important conceptual corollary of this conception of the constitution of human personhood is that 'person' has the conceptual status of a category and not a classification concept. It determines the meaning and range of application of all possible statements about a human person and provides the framework in which statements about what human persons are can be made.[18] This implies that personhood is an ontologically primitive category: it cannot be derived from any other concept and cannot be adequately defined through any other concept. The unique relational constitution of personhood defies any attempt at understanding personhood in terms of the *differentia specifica* of a prior ontological given. Definitions like the classic definition of Boethius of the person as *rationalis naturae individua substantia* are philosophically insufficient and in their theological usage misleading, because they ignore the categorical status of the concept of personhood and its 'primitive' ontological status.[19]

---

[18] Cf. Dalferth/Jüngel op. cit. (note 3), p. 62f.

[19] Boethius' definition of the concept of the person was developed in a christological context in his treatise *Liber de persona et duabus naturis contra Eutychem et Nestorium* (cf. c. 2f. *PL* 64, 1343 BC). In this christological context his main interest is to show that a universal substance cannot be predicated as a person, this predicate can only be applied to individual substances. His main intention is therefore to locate the concept of the person in the traditional classification scheme of the *arbor porphyriana* and to demonstrate its exclusive predicability of individual substances. There is no reflection on any distinction between human and non-human individuals and therefore complete disregard for personal relations as a defining characteristic of the person. Taken out of its christological context Boethius' formula had a 'natural' appeal in a cultural milieu where there were strong tendencies to equate the basic distinction of humanity with rational-

8.   The Church as the community of faith is the personal and communal expression of the recreation of humanity's created sociality as redeemed sociality.

Where the relationship between humanity and God is restored in Christ all the other relationships by which human being is characterized as relational being are restored as well. We have

ity. For the interpretation of Boethius' definition cf. Heribert Mühlen, *Der Heilige Geist als Person*, 4th edition Münster: Aschendorff 1966, pp. 34ff. Richard of St. Victor's conception of the person is often seen as a complementary 'correction' of Boethius' definition. This overlooks that it is formed in a different context and contains a number of revolutionary insights. The context for his definition is that of the doctrine of the Trinity and his decisive argument against Boethius consists in the thesis that God's *nature* is in itself *rationalis naturae individua substantia* so that to accept it as the definition of the person would lead to equating person and nature in the divine being which adds heresy to logical inconsistency. His own proposal *divinae* (or in another connection *intelligibilis*) *naturae incommunicabilis existentia (De Trin. 4,21 PL 196, 845A)* is intended to point to two different issues that are both combined in the concept of *existentia*: the question *what* something is (*quale quid sit*, the *modus essendi*) and *where* it receives its being from (*unde habeat esse*, the *modus obtinendi*). In his explanation Richard relies on a somewhat questionable linguistic and etymological analysis of *ex-sistentia* or *ex-sistere*: *sistere* points to the fact that a person has its existence in itself and not in something else; and *ex* indicates an originating relation which indicates where the person has its being from. Both these aspects are incommunicable in the sense that they cannot be shared or transferred. The singularity of a person is not only rooted in its own exemplification of its substance, but also in its relation to an other from which it originated. Cf. H. Mühlen op. cit. pp. 37-40. Richard combines in this way personal identity and constitution through the other as the defining characteristics of a person. This not only recaptures the main insights of the Cappadocians' reflection on the Trinity, it also indicates the aspects in which personal being differs from all other being: in personal identity and the constitution of this identity through the other. Both aspects cannot be derived from other metaphysical concepts (which is why Richard does not refer to already established metaphysical principles or classification systems in attempting to validate his argument, but points to experience '. . . per experientiam novimus' [4, 414 PL 196, 938D]). For an illuminating comparison of the Boethian (and Cartesian) conception as the person with the alternative understanding of persons in relation, rooted in trinitarian theology cf. C. E. Gunton, 'The One, the Three and the Many'. *Inaugural Lecture King's College London*, 1985, now in: *The Promise of Trinitarian Theology*, Edinburgh: T. & T. Clark 1991, pp. 86-103.

seen that sin as the contradiction against God and as the violation of the relationship between God and humanity immediately affects the interpersonal relationships of humanity. The created sociality of sinful humanity is distorted so that instead of being persons in community human beings are alienated from one another and are even in their social forms of organisation constantly endangered by mutual estrangement. That does not mean that human beings suddenly cease living in social relationships. But in the state of sin the sociality of human being seems to threaten and limit individual personhood and its exercise. If created freedom is abused in contradiction to God's relationship to humanity, community is perceived as a restriction and limitation of freedom instead of its correlate. Where communities are formed they remain partial and exclusive and define themselves in opposition to other social groups. In the perspective of sin the relational existence of humanity is experienced as a threat to human flourishing and not as the ground of its possibility. One of the symptoms of this situation is that we experience ourselves as being in the hands of other people for the determination of our identity and the exercise of our existence. The threatening character of this situation can be explained from the fact that where the relationship of God to humanity is denied, the limitation and determination of our social relationships through the relationship of all human beings to their creator is denied as well, and interpersonal relationships take the form of domination and subordination. In these relationships some human persons assume a superhuman place, with the effect that other persons are turned into instruments for the realization of an alien will. The otherness of the human person and the dignity of human persons is denied and they become extensions of the will of the oppressor.

The church is the place where the recreation of human personhood in the image of Christ is acknowledged in faith as the reconstitution of the created sociality of human being as redeemed sociality.[20] Insofar as the definition of human personhood is seen in conformity with Christ it is understood as being determined by the participation in the relationship of the Son with the Father through the Spirit. The relationship to God which is restored in Christ is in this way perceived as participation in the personal

---

[20] Cf. Daniel Hardy's essay 'Created and Redeemed Sociality' in: Colin E. Gunton and Daniel W. Hardy (eds.), *On Being the Church. Essays on the Christian Community,* Edinburgh: T.&T. Clark, pp. 21-47.

communion of the Trinity — not by nature, but in grace.[21] The relationship of God to humanity and the restored relationship of humanity to God is therefore fundamentally determined by the personal communion which is the mode of being of the divine life.[22] The relationship of persons in communion is therefore the transcendental matrix for the restoration of the divine-human relationship and for the recreation of created sociality as redeemed sociality in the church.

The church is constituted through the divine Word and in the Spirit where the proclamation of the gospel of Christ is authenticated in the Spirit as the truth about the relationship of God and humanity.[23] The content of the Gospel is reflected in the form in which it becomes effective, so that faith as the grateful acknowledgement of the truth of the Gospel documents in its personal and communal character the restoration of the relationship of God and humanity as well as the recreation of personal being in communion as the character of redeemed sociality. The restoration of human personhood in faith is both characterized by the relationship and by the distinction of human persons to the tri-personal God. Where human personhood is reconstituted as conformity with Christ and thereby participates through grace in the personal communion of the divine life, the distinction between divine and human personhood is emphatically reasserted against the attempt of sinful self-interpretation to blur this distinction. The dependence of human personhood on its relationship with the divine persons discloses the categorical difference between the being of the creator and the being of his human creatures. Participation in the Spirit in the Son's relationship to the Father does not make the human person more divine, since the categorical distinction between created being and the being of the creator excludes an understanding of divinity as being capable of instantiation in degrees. Rather, it makes the human person more human, since it restores the created destiny of humanity through conformity with Christ, and thereby destroys the assumption of the status

---

21 For a correction of the 'physical' misunderstanding of this participation cf. Thomas F. Torrance, *The Trinitarian Faith. The Evangelical Theology of the Ancient Catholic Church*, Edinburgh: T.&T. Clark 1988, pp. 188ff.

22 This is developed in Colin Gunton's essay 'The Church on Earth: The Roots of Community', in *On Being the Church* pp. 48-80.

23 The bases of this view in the theology of the Reformers are discussed in my essay 'The Creature of the Word: Recovering the Ecclesiology of the Reformers', in *On Being the Church*, pp. 110-155.

of God which is characteristic for human sin.[24]

All interpersonal human relationships have their criterion in the restored relationship of humanity with God. This has critical as well as constructive implications for human being in the church. The restoration of the relationship between humanity and God discloses all attempts where human beings assume a quasi-divine status over other human beings as attempts at replacing the creator by a human authority. The reconstitution of created sociality in the church is therefore the radical critique of all forms of human relationships determined by domination and oppression. Positively, the reconstitution of created sociality as redeemed sociality is the reconciliation of personal freedom and personal communion. The dialectic between freedom and community is overcome where both freedom and communion are understood as grounded in the relationship of the trinitarian God to humanity who enables human beings to be free in community and to live in community as free agents, since both freedom and community are equally constitutive aspects of human personhood.[25] Freedom, which is grounded in and limited by the relationship to God, and community, which is equally grounded and shaped by the relationship to God, become not only compatible, but can only be jointly realized.

9.   *The Church is called to witness to the recreation of the human person in the image of Christ by proclaiming God's judgement and grace as criticism, promise and commission.*

As the recreation of created sociality the life of redeemed humanity in the Church has universal significance for the whole of humanity. It is, however, necessary to see that the existence of the church as a partial community which defines its identity and character over against other communities will call the universality of the restoration of the relationship between humanity and God in Christ into question, unless its mode of existence is one of constant self-transcendence.[26] As long as there is a 'church'

---

[24] This is forcefully emphasized by Eberhard Jüngel in 'Der Gott entsprechende Mensch', op. cit. (note 3), especially pp. 306-309.

[25] Cf. the illuminating discussion of 'Limitation and Freedom' in Richard Norris 'Human Being' in *Keeping the Faith*, especially pp. 93-98.

[26] For the trinitarian structure of ecclesial self-transcendence cf. Carl Heinz Ratschow, 'Die Lehre von der Kirche. Eine trinitarisch aufgebaute Skizze' in *Von den Wandlungen Gottes*, pp. 244-258.

alongside the 'world' and a 'world' *extra muros ecclesiae* the church does not exist for herself, but for the world. The church can only remain the faithful witness of the universality of the recreation of the human person in Christ, if it proclaims the Gospel of the restoration of the divine-human relationship through Christ and in the Spirit to all the world. The proclamation of the Gospel is therefore not simply one function of the church amongst many others, but its central mark of existence as the witness to the universality of salvation in Christ. The Gospel of the reconciliation of God and the world in Christ has its central content both in God's judgement over the 'old being' of sin and in God's grace in creating the New Being of faith. The proclamation of the Gospel is therefore criticism, promise and commission.

The Gospel is the proclamation of God's judgement over sin, because it identifies all relationships in which human beings exist and which are not grounded in the relationship of God to humanity as forms of contradiction against God's will of grace for his creation. It discloses the self-destructive character of relational being that is dislocated in the structure of relatedness that characterizes the created order. Where the judgement of God over sin is proclaimed in the ministry of the church it relates the criticism of all alienating relationships of human beings to themselves, to one another and to nature to the revolt against God the creator. The forms of estrangement which characterize the factual existence of humanity can thereby be identified as sin. The radical character of this criticism is grounded in the fact that its criterion is not simply the prevention of greater evil and self-destruction, but the overcoming of sin in Christ. The restoration of the relationship of humanity and God will only be a credible standard for the criticism of the church, if it is applied critically to those outside the church as well as self-critically with regard to the church herself where the content of her proclamation is called into question by the forms of her existence.

The Gospel is the proclamation of God's grace as the universal promise for humankind insofar as it not only identifies the contradiction against God as the root of human alienation, but also proclaims the restoration of the relationship of God and humanity as the ground of salvation. In proclaiming the Gospel as God's promise for the salvation of humankind the church can become instrumental for the realization of God's purpose for his creation. The church can, however, not perform this instrumental function by its own achievement so that its proclamation is effective without God's grace. It can only hope and trust that God will authenticate the proclamation of the church through his grace so that people are drawn into the relationship of humanity to God through becoming part of the community of the church.

The criticism of the proclamation of God's judgement and the promise of God's grace in the ministry of the church define the recreated personhood of humanity as commission to relate to all relationships of human being in accordance with the restored relationship of humanity and God. The life of faith that is passively constituted through God's justifying grace is not *vita passiva*, but *vita activa* insofar it is determined by the active response of faith to God's judgement and grace. The Gospel is therefore the commission of the community of the Church to act in the relationship of humanity to nature and in the relationship to culture in such a way that these relationships correspond to the restored divine-human relationship.

10.   The eschatological existence of New Being in the church is exercised by responsible stewardship for the natural world as God's creation.

The recreation of the human person in conformity with Christ is the definitive relocation of human being as relational being in the relational cosmos of God's creation. In the state of sin where human beings assume the status of God, the relationship of humanity to nature becomes one of conflict, because human beings are displaced in the world of nature. At the same time the natural world is involved in the Fall of human beings, insofar as the relationship of humanity to nature disturbs the created order in such a way that it ceases to be the beneficial natural foundation of human existence. This is clearly witnessed today by the fact that the human exploitation of the natural environment and the unrestricted domination over nature puts the natural foundations of human life at risk.[27]

The relocation of human relational being in Christ and through the Spirit involves the recognition of the whole natural world, including human life, as God's creation. This limits the relationship of human beings to nature in such a way that in all our interaction with nature God is acknowledged and respected as its creator. At the same time, human beings are called to contribute to the flourishing of the whole natural creation in responsible stewardship for God's creation. This implies relating to the natural order in such a way that the flourishing of the natural order and of

[27] Cf. John Zizioulas, 'Preserving God's Creation. Three Lectures on Theology and Ecology', *King's Theological Review* XII (1989) and XIII (1990).

human persons are recognized as being mutually interdependent. The specific personal status of human beings in creation as the images of God implies that the response to God the creator in the exercise of human personhood comprises all relations in which human being is intrinsically related to the natural order.

In this context it has to be emphasized that the image of God is restored as the recreation of created sociality as redeemed sociality where the image of God finds it expression in persons in community. This means for the restored relationship of humanity to nature that human beings are called to relate to nature as persons in community. This prevents the specific relationship of one group of humanity to nature from being permitted to be destructive for the relationship of another group of people to nature (as it is witnessed today in the effects of the agricultural exploitation of countries of the Two-Thirds-World through the industrial nations). And it also excludes the restriction of the chances and quality of the life of future generations through the reckless relationship of a former generation to nature (as it is documented by the use of nuclear energy in the present generation and its legacy for later generations). It is here, in the interaction of the sociality of human relational being and its dependence on its relationship to nature that the implications of theological anthropology for the prospect of an ethic of createdness begin to emerge.

11. The life of faith is practised in participation in the world of culture as the field where human persons act as God's co-creators.

The specific form of the image of God as the relational being of free persons in community determines human being as 'by nature', that is, in virtue of the specific relationship of the triune God to humanity, cultural being. Freedom and sociality as the distinctive characteristics of human personhood determine the relationship of humanity to nature as cultural activity. They determine the relationship of humanity to nature as one shaped by free intentional action and not by an instinctual stimulus-response mechanism, and they create the space where human beings can extend their natural means of action through cultural instruments (from blunt tools to supertechnology). The sociality of human personhood furthermore necessitates the development of symbolic means of interaction (language) in order to make joint action and communal experience possible. After the Fall these specific characteristics of personal relational being continue to exist in their empty form without the orientation they receive from the relationship of humanity to God. Insofar as they participate in the disorientation of sin, these characteristics of human being as cultural being are ambiguous and are the form of destruction as much as of creativity.

To characterize the cultural existence of human persons in community by the concept of co-creatorship is not entirely unproblematical. Co-creatorship means neither that human creativity somehow completes the work that God the creator has left unfinished, nor that God's creativity and human creativity cooperate on the same level. Human co-creatorship as the cultural expression of the recreation of the image of God in faith is based on the recognition that the triune God is the ground of human freedom and community which are the marks of human personhood in the image of God. Human cultural activity therefore receives its limitation and criterion from the relationship of God to humanity. It is on the basis of this relationship and distinction that cultural activity can be understood as cooperation with God in the achievement of the fellowship of God with the whole of his creation in the Kingdom of God.

The church is called to participate in the world of culture, because the separation of church and culture as well as the segmentation of culture is itself symptomatic of the disorientation of sin where the relationship of God to humanity is not acknowledged as the foundation of all relationships in which humanity exists. The restoration of this relationship in the recreation of human personhood in community as the universal reconstitution of human relational being is therefore the ground for the eschatological overcoming of the separation between church and culture and the eschatological impetus for the unity of culture. The segmentation of culture documents the fact that human culture disintegrates in separate and conflicting autonomous spheres where human cultural activity is not seen as grounded in God's relationship to the world, so that all attempts at reconstituting the unity of culture apart from this relationship result in a state of heteronomy that subjects one cultural sphere to the rule of another. Insofar as the church witnesses to the universal significance of the recreation of the human person in Christ, it points to the relationship of God to his creation as the theonomous ground of the unity of culture and of the reconciliation of the church and culture in the eschatological community of the Kingdom of God.[28]

[28] Paul Tillich's programme for a theology of culture still remains one of the most creative stimuli for a contemporary theology of culture. Cf. Paul Tillich, *Main Works — Hauptwerke, vol. II: Writings in the Philosophy of Culture* (ed. Michael Palmer), Berlin-New York: de Gruyter 1989.

12.   *The community of faith in the church is the anticipation of and witness to the perfect fulfilment of the fellowship of the triune God with his creation in the Kingdom of God.*